I0815316

Editorial project:
© 2025 **booq** publishing, S.L.
c/ Domènech, 7-9, 2° 1ª
08012 Barcelona, Spain
T: +34 93 268 80 88
www.booqpublishing.com

ISBN: 978-84-9936-601-2 [EN]
ISBN: 978-84-9936-575-6 [ES]

© Éditions du Layeur
Dépôt Légal : Mai 2025
Espagne, en mai 2025

ISBN : 978-2-38378-079-3

Editorial coordinator:
Claudia Martínez Alonso

Art director:
Mireia Casanovas Soley

Editor:
Daniela Santos Quartino

Layout:
Cristina Simó Perales

Translation:
© **booq** publishing, S.L.

Printing in Spain

More than just a decorative resource, color is a language that defines the personality of spaces and a catalyst that influences the mood and energy of those who inhabit them. Every hue has the power to transform environments—evoking calm and introspection as well as vitality and dynamism.

Designers strategically use color to modify the perception of spaces. Warm tones can make a room feel more inviting and vibrant, while cool shades—such as green and blue—bring serenity and a sense of spaciousness. The color palette is a key decision that articulates the relationship between volumes, light, and textures.

Iconic examples in 20th-century architecture reflect the diverse approaches to color. Luis Barragán used it to enhance the emotional impact of spaces, while Álvaro Siza opted for achromatic neutrality. Lina Bo Bardi introduced red into structural elements, and Ricardo Legorreta immersed himself in the vibrant tones of Mexican culture.

The projects presented in this book explore this chromatic richness from different perspectives. In each one, color takes center stage—whether through bold contrasts, immersive palettes, or tonal subtleties that add depth and warmth. These are spaces designed to be lived in, where every color choice leaves a mark and contributes to the home's identity. Pure emotion.

Mehr als nur ein dekoratives Element ist Farbe eine Sprache, die die Persönlichkeit von Räumen definiert, sowie ein Katalysator, der die Stimmung und Energie der Bewohner beeinflusst. Jede Nuance hat die Kraft, Atmosphären zu verwandeln – von Ruhe und Introspektion bis hin zu Vitalität und Dynamik.

Designer setzen Farbe strategisch ein, um die Wahrnehmung von Räumen zu verändern. Warme Töne können einen Raum einladender und lebendiger wirken lassen, während kühlere Farben wie Grün und Blau Gelassenheit und Weite vermitteln. Die Farbpalette ist eine zentrale Entscheidung, die das Zusammenspiel von Volumen, Licht und Texturen bestimmt.

Ikonische Beispiele der Architektur des 20. Jahrhunderts spiegeln die Vielfalt der Farbverwendung wider. Luis Barragán nutzte Farbe, um emotionale Räume zu schaffen, während Álvaro Siza auf eine achromatische Neutralität setzte. Lina Bo Bardi integrierte Rot in strukturelle Elemente, und Ricardo Legorreta tauchte in die lebendigen Farbtöne der mexikanischen Kultur ein.

Die in diesem Buch präsentierten Projekte erforschen diese chromatische Vielfalt aus verschiedenen Perspektiven. In jedem ist Farbe der Protagonist – sei es durch kühne Kontraste, einhüllende Paletten oder subtile Tonänderungen, die Tiefe und Wärme verleihen. Diese Räume sind zum Leben entworfen, in denen jede Farbwahl eine Spur hinterlässt und zur Identität des Zuhauses beiträgt. Pure Emotion.

Plus qu'une ressource décorative, la couleur est un langage qui définit la personnalité des espaces et un catalyseur qui influence l'humeur et l'énergie de ceux qui les habitent. Chaque nuance a le pouvoir de transformer les environnements, d'évoquer le calme et l'introspection, mais aussi la vitalité et le dynamisme.

Les designers utilisent la couleur de manière stratégique pour modifier la perception des espaces. Les tons chauds peuvent rendre une pièce plus accueillante et plus vivante, tandis que les tons froids — tels que le vert et le bleu — apportent sérénité et espace. La palette de couleurs est une décision clé qui articule la relation entre les volumes, la lumière et les textures.

Des exemples emblématiques de l'architecture du XXe siècle reflètent la diversité des approches de l'utilisation de la couleur. Luis Barragán l'a utilisée pour renforcer l'émotion des espaces, Álvaro Siza a opté pour une neutralité achromatique. Lina Bo Bardi a introduit le rouge dans les éléments structurels, et Ricardo Legorreta s'est immergé dans les tons vibrants de la culture mexicaine.

Les projets présentés dans ce livre explorent cette richesse chromatique sous différentes perspectives. Dans chacun d'eux, la couleur occupe une place centrale, que ce soit par des contrastes audacieux, des palettes enveloppantes ou des subtilités tonales qui ajoutent de la profondeur et de la chaleur. Ce sont des espaces conçus pour être habités, où chaque choix chromatique laisse une trace et contribue à l'identité de la maison. L'émotion à l'état pur.

Más que un recurso decorativo, el color es un lenguaje que define la personalidad de los espacios y un catalizador que influye en el estado de ánimo y la energía de quienes los habitan. Cada tono tiene el poder de transformar los ambientes; de evocar la calma y la introspección pero también la vitalidad y el dinamismo.

Los diseñadores emplean el color de manera estratégica para modificar la percepción de los espacios. Los tonos cálidos pueden hacer que una habitación resulte más acogedora y vibrante, mientras que los fríos —como el verde y el azul— le traen serenidad y amplitud. La paleta cromática es una decisión clave que articula la relación entre volúmenes, luz y texturas.

Ejemplos icónicos en la arquitectura del siglo XX reflejan la diversidad de enfoques en el uso del color. Luis Barragán lo empleó para potenciar la emoción de los espacios, Álvaro Siza opta por la neutralidad acromática. Lina Bo Bardi introdujo el rojo en elementos estructurales, y Ricardo Legorreta se sumergió en los tonos vibrantes de la cultura mexicana.

Los proyectos que se presentan en este libro exploran esta riqueza cromática desde distintas perspectivas. En cada uno, el color es protagonista, ya sea a través de contrastes audaces, paletas envolventes o sutilezas tonales que aportan profundidad y calidez. Son espacios diseñados para ser vividos, donde cada elección cromática deja una huella y contribuye a la identidad del hogar. Pura emoción.

ARABELLA ROCCA DESIGN

CASA VERDE >

ROME, ITALY

Photos: © Daniele Vergari, Ingrid Taro

CASA VERDE

Casa Verde takes its name from the predominant tone in this flat located in a nature-rich urban area in Rome, where greenery spreads uninterruptedly. The central idea was to create a harmonious fusion between the interior of the home and its surroundings, transforming the living area into a continuous space with the lush landscape outside, visible through the large windows.
The design reflects the vision of architect Arabella Rocca, with balanced tones. The skilful choice of vibrant colours reflects the personality of the clients, always maintaining a balance between elegance and a touch of pop style, without sacrificing harmony in the details. The living area is a large open space, designed for conviviality and social interaction, similar to a small urban square with uniform elements that frame daily life. The night area is organised into several private rooms (master suite, children's rooms, bathrooms), separated from the public area by a large foyer. Each space presents different styles and colours, adapted to daily needs, creating a balance between aesthetics and functionality.

Casa Verde ist nach dem vorherrschenden Farbton in dieser Wohnung benannt, die sich in einem naturreichen Stadtgebiet in Rom befindet, wo sich ununterbrochen Grünflächen ausbreiten. Die zentrale Idee war es, eine harmonische Verschmelzung zwischen dem Inneren des Hauses und seiner Umgebung zu schaffen und den Wohnbereich in einen durchgehenden Raum mit der üppigen Landschaft draußen zu verwandeln, die durch die großen Fenster sichtbar ist.
Das Design spiegelt die Vision der Architektin Arabella Rocca wider, mit ausgewogenen Farbtönen. Die geschickte Wahl der leuchtenden Farben spiegelt die Persönlichkeit der Bauherren wider, wobei stets ein Gleichgewicht zwischen Eleganz und einem Hauch von Pop-Stil gewahrt wird, ohne dass die Harmonie der Details darunter leidet. Der Wohnbereich ist ein großer offener Raum, der für Geselligkeit und soziale Interaktion konzipiert wurde, ähnlich einem kleinen städtischen Platz mit einheitlichen Elementen, die das tägliche Leben einrahmen. Der Nachtbereich ist in mehrere private Räume unterteilt (Master-Suite, Kinderzimmer, Bäder), die durch ein großes Foyer vom öffentlichen Bereich getrennt sind. Jeder Raum weist unterschiedliche Stile und Farben auf, die an die täglichen Bedürfnisse angepasst sind und ein Gleichgewicht zwischen Ästhetik und Funktionalität schaffen.

Casa Verde tire son nom de la tonalité prédominante de cet appartement situé dans une zone urbaine de Rome riche en nature, où la verdure s'étend de manière ininterrompue. L'idée centrale était de créer une fusion harmonieuse entre l'intérieur de la maison et son environnement, en transformant la zone de vie en un espace continu avec le paysage luxuriant à l'extérieur, visible à travers les grandes fenêtres.
Le design reflète la vision de l'architecte Arabella Rocca, avec des tons équilibrés. Le choix habile de couleurs vives reflète la personnalité des clients, en maintenant toujours un équilibre entre l'élégance et une touche de style pop, sans sacrifier l'harmonie dans les détails. La zone de vie est un grand espace ouvert, conçu pour la convivialité et l'interaction sociale, semblable à une petite place urbaine avec des éléments uniformes qui encadrent la vie quotidienne. L'espace nuit est organisé en plusieurs pièces privées (suite parentale, chambres d'enfants, salles de bains), séparées de l'espace public par un grand foyer. Chaque espace présente des styles et des couleurs différents, adaptés aux besoins quotidiens, créant un équilibre entre esthétique et fonctionnalité.

Casa Verde toma su nombre del tono predominante en este apartamento ubicado en una zona urbana con mucha naturaleza en Roma, donde el verdor se extiende de manera ininterrumpida. La idea central fue crear una fusión armónica entre el interior de la vivienda y el entorno, transformando la zona de estar en un espacio continuo con el exuberante paisaje exterior, visible a través de las grandes ventanas.
El diseño refleja la visión de la arquitecta Arabella Rocca, con tonos equilibrados. La elección hábil de colores vibrantes refleja la personalidad de los clientes, manteniendo siempre un equilibrio entre elegancia y un toque de estilo pop, sin sacrificar la armonía en los detalles. La zona de estar es un gran espacio abierto, pensado para la convivencia y la interacción social, similar a una pequeña plaza urbana con elementos uniformes que enmarcan la vida diaria. El área de noche está organizada en varias estancias privadas (suite principal, habitaciones para niños, baños), separadas de la zona pública por un amplio vestíbulo. Cada espacio presenta diferentes estilos y colores, adaptados a las necesidades diarias, creando un equilibrio entre la estética y la funcionalidad.

Vibrant colors reflect the clients' personality, balancing elegance with a pop style, while preserving harmony in the details.

ATELIER GERMAIN

PROJET LEMAÎTRE >

NANTERRE, PARIS

Photos: © Laura Jacques

PROJET LEMAÎTRE

The transformation of this house on the outskirts of Paris is a tribute to color and creativity. With a vision inspired by Arty Pop, vibrant tones, graphic patterns, and artistic pieces were used to turn a traditional home into a dynamic and welcoming space.
Before the intervention, the house had a classic, compartmentalized layout with a narrow, impractical kitchen. The solution was clear: open up the spaces and enhance natural light. By removing the central wall, a strong visual connection was created between the kitchen, entrance, and staircase, allowing for fluid circulation and a more sociable atmosphere. Color is the project's unifying theme. Walls and furniture are adorned with bold, contrasting hues, evoking the pop aesthetic of the 1960s and 70s. Rounded openings soften the space's geometry, while graphic motifs add a visual rhythm. The result is a home full of character. Here, color is not just a decorative element but a tool for sculpting space and evoking emotions, achieving a balance between functionality and a bold visual identity.

Die Umgestaltung dieses Hauses am Stadtrand von Paris ist eine Hommage an Farbe und Kreativität. Inspiriert vom Arty-Pop-Stil wurde eine Palette lebendiger Töne, grafischer Muster und künstlerischer Elemente verwendet, um ein traditionelles Haus in eine dynamische und einladende Umgebung zu verwandeln.
Vor der Renovierung war das Haus klassisch geschnitten und stark unterteilt, mit einer engen und wenig funktionalen Küche. Die Lösung war naheliegend: Die Räume öffnen und mehr Licht einlassen. Durch den Abriss der zentralen Wand entstand eine großzügige visuelle Achse zwischen Küche, Eingangsbereich und Treppe, die eine fließende Zirkulation und eine geselligere Atmosphäre ermöglicht. Farbe ist der rote Faden des Projekts. Wände und Möbel wurden mit mutigen Kontrasten gestaltet und erinnern an den Pop-Art-Stil der 1960er- und 1970er-Jahre. Abgerundete Durchgänge mildern die Geometrie des Raumes, während grafische Muster eine dynamische Struktur verleihen. Das Ergebnis ist ein Haus voller Charakter, in dem Farbe nicht nur dekoratives Element, sondern ein Werkzeug zur Gestaltung von Raum und Emotionen ist. Es entsteht eine Balance zwischen Funktionalität und einer kraftvollen visuellen Identität.

La transformation de cette maison de la banlieue parisienne est un hommage à la couleur et à la créativité. Avec une vision inspirée d'Arty Pop, des tons vibrants, des motifs graphiques et des pièces artistiques ont été utilisés pour transformer une maison traditionnelle en un environnement dynamique et accueillant.
Avant l'intervention, la maison présentait un agencement classique et cloisonné, avec une cuisine exiguë et peu fonctionnelle. La solution était claire : ouvrir les espaces et maximiser la lumière. En supprimant le mur central, un grand axe de communication visuelle a été créé entre la cuisine, l'entrée et l'escalier, permettant une circulation fluide et une atmosphère plus sociable. L'utilisation de la couleur est le fil conducteur du projet. Les murs et le mobilier sont habillés de teintes vives et contrastées, évoquant l'esthétique pop des années 60 et 70. Les ouvertures arrondies adoucissent la géométrie de l'espace, tandis que les motifs graphiques donnent un rythme visuel. Le résultat est une maison pleine de caractère. Ici, la couleur n'est pas seulement un élément décoratif, mais un outil pour sculpter l'espace et susciter des émotions, en trouvant un équilibre entre la fonctionnalité et une identité visuelle audacieuse.

La transformación de esta casa en las afueras de París es un homenaje al color y la creatividad. Con una visión inspirada en el Arty Pop, se han empleado tonos vibrantes, patrones gráficos y piezas artísticas para convertir una vivienda tradicional en un entorno dinámico y acogedor.
Antes de la intervención, la casa contaba con una distribución clásica y compartimentada, con una cocina estrecha y poco funcional. La solución fue clara: abrir los espacios y potenciar la luminosidad. Al eliminar la pared central, se creó un gran eje de comunicación visual entre la cocina, la entrada y la escalera, permitiendo una circulación fluida y un ambiente más sociable. El uso del color es el hilo conductor del proyecto. Las paredes y los muebles se visten con matices audaces y de contraste, evocando la estética pop de los años 60 y 70. Aperturas redondeadas suavizan la geometría del espacio, mientras que motivos gráficos aportan un ritmo visual. El resultado es una casa llena de carácter. Aquí, el color no es solo un elemento decorativo, sino una herramienta para esculpir el espacio y despertar emociones, logrando un equilibrio entre funcionalidad y una identidad visual audaz.

Arty Pop inspiration transforms a traditional home with vibrant tones, graphic patterns, and art pieces into a dynamic space.

ATELIER ND INTERIOR

FAMILY RETREAT >

LOENEN AAN DE VECHT, THE NETHERLANDS

Photos: © Space Content Studio

FAMILY RETREAT

The aesthetic of this countryside retreat balances the serenity of its idyllic location along the Vecht River with a vibrant and sophisticated style. The color palette not only dialogues with the original architecture but also enhances the warmth of the wooden beams, the texture of the thatched roof, and the fluidity of the spaces. From boldly patterned fabrics to the kitchen's marble surfaces, every visual choice contributes to a transformation that blends timeless elegance with an unexpected twist. The designers at Atelier ND Interior have left their signature touch by incorporating textures and pieces with African influences, alongside textiles from Pierre Frey, Beata Heuman, and Helene Blanche. The bedroom evokes a safari lodge, while the kitchen—clad in Calacatta Viola marble—serves as the visual centerpiece of the home. British countryside-inspired details, such as vintage lamps and gathered curtain fronts on cabinets, reinforce the cozy atmosphere.
Unlike the owners' Amsterdam apartment, dominated by a bold orange tone, the aesthetic here is more restrained—though not without statement pieces: a curved red sofa, built-in cabinetry, and a selection of wallpaper designs that add depth and dynamism.

Die Ästhetik dieses ländlichen Refugiums balanciert die Ruhe der idyllischen Umgebung des Flusses Vecht mit einem lebendigen und raffinierten Stil. Die Farbpalette harmoniert nicht nur mit der ursprünglichen Architektur, sondern betont auch die Wärme der Holzbalken, die Textur des Reetdachs und die fließenden Räume. Von kühnen Mustern in Stoffen bis hin zu Marmor in der Küche – jede visuelle Wahl trägt zu einer Transformation bei, die das Zeitlose mit einer unerwarteten Note verbindet. Die Designerinnen von Atelier ND Interior haben ihre unverwechselbare Handschrift hinterlassen, indem sie Texturen und Stücke mit afrikanischen Einflüssen integrierten, neben Stoffen von Pierre Frey, Beata Heuman und Helene Blanche. Das Schlafzimmer erinnert an eine Safari-Lodge, während die mit Calacatta-Viola-Marmor verkleidete Küche das visuelle Herzstück des Hauses bildet. Inspiriert von der britischen Landhausästhetik verstärken Vintage-Lampen und geraffte Vorhänge an den Schränken die gemütliche Atmosphäre.
Im Gegensatz zur Amsterdamer Wohnung der Besitzer, die von einem kräftigen Orangeton dominiert wird, ist die Ästhetik hier zurückhaltender – aber dennoch mit markanten Akzenten: ein geschwungenes rotes Sofa, maßgefertigte Einbauschränke und eine Auswahl an Tapeten, die Tiefe und Dynamik verleihen.

L'esthétique de ce refuge de campagne concilie la sérénité du cadre idyllique de la rivière Vecht avec un style vibrant et sophistiqué. Non seulement la palette de couleurs dialogue avec l'architecture d'origine, mais elle met également en valeur la chaleur des poutres en bois, la texture du toit de chaume et la fluidité des espaces. Des tissus aux motifs audacieux au marbre de la cuisine, chaque choix visuel contribue à une transformation qui allie l'intemporalité à une touche inattendue. Les designers de l'Atelier ND Interior ont ajouté leur empreinte distinctive en incorporant des textures et des pièces d'influence africaine, ainsi que des textiles de Pierre Frey, Beata Heuman et Helene Blanche. La chambre à coucher évoque un pavillon de safari, tandis que la cuisine, revêtue de marbre Calacatta Viola, est l'épicentre visuel de la maison. Des détails inspirés de la campagne britannique, tels que des lampes vintage et des rideaux à volants dans les armoires, renforcent l'atmosphère chaleureuse.
Contrairement à l'appartement des propriétaires à Amsterdam, qui est dominé par une teinte orange audacieuse, l'esthétique est ici plus sobre, mais avec des touches frappantes : un canapé rouge incurvé, des armoires encastrées et une sélection de papiers peints ajoutent de la profondeur et du dynamisme.

La estética de este refugio campestre equilibra la serenidad del entorno idílico del río Vecht con un estilo vibrante y sofisticado. La paleta cromática no solo dialoga con la arquitectura original, también potencia la calidez de las vigas de madera, la textura del tejado de paja y la fluidez de los espacios. Desde telas con estampados audaces hasta el mármol de la cocina, cada elección visual contribuye a una transformación que combina lo atemporal con un toque inesperado. Las diseñadoras de Atelier ND Interior han aportado su sello distintivo, incorporando texturas y piezas con influencias africanas, además de textiles de Pierre Frey, Beata Heuman y Helene Blanche. El dormitorio evoca un lodge de safari, mientras que la cocina, revestida en mármol Calacatta Viola, es el epicentro visual de la casa. Detalles inspirados en la campiña británica, como lámparas vintage y cortinas fruncidas en los armarios, refuerzan la atmósfera acogedora.
A diferencia del apartamento de los propietarios en Ámsterdam, dominado por un audaz tono naranja, aquí la estética es más contenida, aunque con toques llamativos: un sofá rojo curvo, armarios integrados y una selección de papeles pintados que añaden profundidad y dinamismo.

The aesthetic of this countryside retreat balances the serenity of an idyllic setting with a vibrant and sophisticated style.

ROCKY

BCONNECTED REAL ESTATE, ARCHITECTURE & INTERIOR DESIGN

L.A. VIBES IN MALLORCA >

MALLORCA, SPAIN

Photos: © bconnected

L.A. VIBES IN MALLORCA

Color is the main protagonist of this home, where every room radiates energy and personality. Designed for a young couple with a cosmopolitan vision, the house is a fusion of global influences and an authentic expression of their dynamic lifestyle. After years of living in different countries, the owners settled in Mallorca and actively participated in the creative process of their first permanent home.
The design is an example of bconnected's bold and innovative approach, featuring an energetic chromatic combination enriched with a carefully selected range of textures and a balance between contemporary pieces and vintage elements. The interaction of these materials and objects adds depth to the spaces, creating vibrant yet welcoming environments. The home not only reflects a bold and uncompromising approach to design but also a way of understanding the home as a unique and meaningful refuge. This project showcases how the use of color, the mixing of styles, and attention to detail can shape a space with its own identity, where creativity and comfort coexist in perfect harmony.

Farbe ist der große Protagonist dieses Hauses, in dem jeder Raum Energie und Persönlichkeit ausstrahlt. Entworfen für ein junges Paar mit einer kosmopolitischen Vision, ist das Haus eine Fusion globaler Einflüsse und ein authentischer Ausdruck ihres dynamischen Lebensstils. Nach Jahren des Lebens in verschiedenen Ländern ließen sich die Eigentümer auf Mallorca nieder und beteiligten sich aktiv am kreativen Prozess ihres ersten dauerhaften Zuhauses.
Das Design ist ein Beispiel für den kühnen und innovativen Ansatz von bconnected und setzt auf eine energetische Farbkombination, bereichert durch eine sorgfältige Auswahl an Texturen und das Gleichgewicht zwischen zeitgenössischen Stücken und Vintage-Elementen. Die Interaktion dieser Materialien und Objekte verleiht den Räumen Tiefe und schafft eine Atmosphäre, die zugleich lebendig und einladend ist. Das Haus spiegelt nicht nur einen mutigen und kompromisslosen Designansatz wider, sondern auch eine Art, das Zuhause als einzigartigen und bedeutungsvollen Rückzugsort zu verstehen. Dieses Projekt zeigt, wie der Einsatz von Farbe, die Mischung verschiedener Stile und die Liebe zum Detail einen Raum mit einer eigenen Identität formen können, in dem Kreativität und Komfort in perfekter Harmonie koexistieren.

La couleur est la grande protagoniste de cette maison, où chaque pièce rayonne d'énergie et de personnalité. Conçue pour un jeune couple à la vision cosmopolite, la maison est une fusion d'influences mondiales et une expression authentique de leur style de vie dynamique. Après avoir vécu dans plusieurs pays, les propriétaires se sont installés à Majorque et ont participé activement au processus créatif de leur premier foyer permanent.
Le design est un exemple de l'approche audacieuse et innovante de Bconnected, misant sur une combinaison chromatique énergique, enrichie par une sélection minutieuse de textures et un équilibre entre pièces contemporaines et éléments vintage. L'interaction entre ces matériaux et objets confère une profondeur aux espaces, créant des ambiances à la fois vibrantes et chaleureuses. Cette maison ne reflète pas seulement une approche audacieuse et assumée du design, mais aussi une manière de concevoir le foyer comme un refuge unique et chargé de sens. Ce projet illustre comment l'usage de la couleur, le mélange des styles et l'attention aux détails peuvent donner naissance à un espace à l'identité propre, où créativité et confort coexistent en parfaite harmonie.

El color es el gran protagonista de esta vivienda, donde cada estancia irradia energía y personalidad. Diseñada para una joven pareja con una visión cosmopolita, la casa es una fusión de influencias globales y una expresión auténtica de su dinámico estilo de vida. Tras años viviendo en distintos países, los propietarios se establecieron en Mallorca y participaron activamente en el proceso creativo de su primer hogar permanente.
El diseño es un ejemplo del enfoque audaz e innovador de bconnected, y apuesta por una energética combinación cromática, enriquecida con una cuidada selección de texturas y el equilibrio entre piezas contemporáneas y elementos vintage. La interacción de estos materiales y objetos otorga profundidad a los espacios, generando ambientes vibrantes y acogedores a la vez. La vivienda no solo refleja un enfoque atrevido y sin concesiones en el diseño, sino también una manera de entender el hogar como un refugio único y lleno de significado. Este proyecto es una muestra de cómo el uso del color, la mezcla de estilos y la atención a los detalles pueden dar forma a un espacio con identidad propia, donde creatividad y confort conviven en perfecta armonía.

SPLENDOR
COSTA SMERALDA
GYPSET

GYPSET

The design reflects bconnected's bold approach, blending energetic colors, textures, and a mix of contemporary and vintage elements.

BEDEL INTERIORS

VILLA IN MARRAKESH >

MARRAKESH, MOROCCO

Photos: © Benoit Diacre

VILLA IN MARRAKESH

Bedel Interiors completely renovated this residence in the Palmeraie in Marrakesh so that its owners could enjoy it for part of the year and welcome family and friends. With 1000 m^2, the house combines modernity and tradition, emphasising the connection with the environment and the use of natural light. The renovation, which began in 2021 and lasted two years, reconfigured the spaces to open up the house to the extensive garden and swimming pool. Local techniques such as pisé, dess on the floors, zelliges tiles and tataoui woven ceiling were used, rescuing Moroccan craftsmanship with a contemporary approach. One of the most striking features was the use of tadelakt lime cladding on all the walls, with a single shade per room on walls, ceilings and floors. Catherine and Kelly Bedel chose warm colours inspired by local spices, such as the ochre of cumin, the red of paprika and the brown of cinnamon, creating welcoming and vibrant environments. The kitchen, bathrooms and living room were completely redesigned, incorporating bespoke oak furniture and pieces selected in Europe. Natural materials and meticulous finishes defined a sophisticated and timeless aesthetic, in dialogue with the essence of this Moroccan city.

Bedel Interiors hat dieses Haus in der Palmeraie von Marrakesch komplett renoviert, damit seine Besitzer es einen Teil des Jahres genießen und Familie und Freunde empfangen können. Das 1000 m^2 große Haus verbindet Modernität und Tradition, wobei die Verbindung mit der Umgebung und die Nutzung des natürlichen Lichts im Vordergrund stehen. Bei der Renovierung, die 2021 begann und zwei Jahre dauerte, wurden die Räume neu gestaltet, um das Haus zum weitläufigen Garten und zum Swimmingpool hin zu öffnen. Lokale Techniken wie Pisé, Dess auf den Böden, zellige Fliesen und gewebte Tataoui-Decken wurden verwendet, um die marokkanische Handwerkskunst mit einem modernen Ansatz zu retten. Eines der auffälligsten Merkmale war die Verwendung von Tadelakt-Kalkverkleidungen an allen Wänden, mit einem einzigen Farbton pro Raum an Wänden, Decken und Böden. Catherine und Kelly Bedel wählten warme Farben, die von lokalen Gewürzen inspiriert sind, wie das Ocker von Kreuzkümmel, das Rot von Paprika und das Braun von Zimt, und schufen so eine einladende und lebendige Umgebung. Die Küche, die Bäder und das Wohnzimmer wurden komplett neu gestaltet und mit maßgefertigten Eichenmöbeln und in Europa ausgewählten Stücken ausgestattet. Natürliche Materialien und eine sorgfältige Verarbeitung sorgten für eine anspruchsvolle und zeitlose Ästhetik, die im Dialog mit dem Wesen dieser marokkanischen Stadt steht.

Bedel Interiors a entièrement rénové cette résidence de la Palmeraie à Marrakech afin que ses propriétaires puissent en profiter une partie de l'année et accueillir famille et amis. D'une superficie de 1000 m^2, la maison allie modernité et tradition, en mettant l'accent sur le lien avec l'environnement et l'utilisation de la lumière naturelle. La rénovation, qui a débuté en 2021 et a duré deux ans, a permis de reconfigurer les espaces afin d'ouvrir la maison sur le vaste jardin et la piscine. Des techniques locales telles que le pisé, le dess sur les sols, les carreaux de zelliges et le plafond tissé tataoui ont été utilisées, sauvant l'artisanat marocain avec une approche contemporaine. L'une des caractéristiques les plus frappantes est l'utilisation d'un revêtement en tadelakt à la chaux sur tous les murs, avec une seule teinte par pièce sur les murs, les plafonds et les sols. Catherine et Kelly Bedel ont choisi des couleurs chaudes inspirées des épices locales, telles que l'ocre du cumin, le rouge du paprika et le brun de la cannelle, créant ainsi des environnements accueillants et dynamiques. La cuisine, les salles de bains et le salon ont été entièrement repensés, intégrant des meubles en chêne sur mesure et des pièces sélectionnées en Europe. Des matériaux naturels et des finitions soignées ont défini une esthétique sophistiquée et intemporelle, en dialogue avec l'essence de cette ville marocaine.

Bedel Interiors renovó por completo esta residencia en la Palmeraie de Marrakech para que sus propietarios pudieran disfrutarla una parte del año y recibir a familiares y amigos. Con 1000 m^2, la vivienda combina modernidad y tradición, destacando la conexión con el entorno y el aprovechamiento de la luz natural. La reforma que se inició en 2021 y se extendió por dos años, reconfiguró los espacios para abrir la casa al extenso jardín y la piscina. Se emplearon técnicas locales como el pisé, el dess en los suelos, los azulejos zelliges y el techo tejido en tataoui, rescatando la artesanía marroquí con un enfoque contemporáneo. Una de las características más destacadas fue el uso del revestimiento de cal tadelakt en todos los muros, con una única tonalidad por habitación en muros, techos y suelos. Catherine y Kelly Bedel eligieron colores cálidos inspirados en las especias locales, como el ocre del comino, el rojo del paprika y el marrón de la canela, creando ambientes acogedores y vibrantes. La cocina, los baños y el salón fueron completamente rediseñados, incorporando mobiliario en roble hecho a medida y piezas seleccionadas en Europa. Materiales naturales y acabados meticulosos definieron una estética sofisticada y atemporal, en diálogo con la esencia de esta ciudad marroquí.

The designers used warm, spice-inspired colors like cumin ochre, paprika red, and cinnamon brown to create cozy, vibrant spaces.

BLANCA ROSA GUTIÉRREZ: ARQUITECTURA, INTERIORISMO Y DISEÑO

PURE CHROMATISM IN MADRID >

MADRID, SPAIN

Photos: © Pablo Sarabia

PURE CHROMATISM IN MADRID

Surprise awaits in every corner of this home, where design transcends the functional to become a sensorial experience. Here, colour is not a simple complement, but the guiding thread of a vibrant and dynamic atmosphere. The new layout resulting from a refurbishment is committed to spaciousness and fluidity, breaking down visual barriers to enhance the connection between the common spaces.
The living room is highlighted by an orange pillar that acts as a focal point. This vibrant tone is balanced by the serenity of an artwork reflecting a deep blue landscape, creating a harmonious contrast with the warm tones of the industrial bamboo floor, the yellow chairs in the dining room and the pink curtains, which soften the atmosphere. The kitchen, bold in its deep blue colour, combines geometric patterns that evoke the freshness of the Mediterranean, while natural wood details soften the whole. The teenagers' washroom is an explosion of yellow, while the master bathroom is identified by deep blue tones and wooden details. The access to the master bedroom is marked by panelling in a deep, warm pink that conveys a sense of cosiness and induces calm.

In diesem Haus, in dem das Design über das Funktionale hinausgeht und zu einer sinnlichen Erfahrung wird, gibt es in jeder Ecke Überraschungen. Hier ist die Farbe nicht einfach nur eine Ergänzung, sondern der rote Faden für eine lebendige und dynamische Atmosphäre. Der neue Grundriss, der aus einer Renovierung hervorgegangen ist, setzt auf Großzügigkeit und Fließfähigkeit und baut visuelle Barrieren ab, um die Verbindung zwischen den Gemeinschaftsräumen zu verbessern.
Das Wohnzimmer wird durch eine orangefarbene Säule hervorgehoben, die als Brennpunkt dient. Dieser leuchtende Ton wird durch die Gelassenheit eines Kunstwerks ausgeglichen, das eine tiefblaue Landschaft widerspiegelt und einen harmonischen Kontrast zu den warmen Tönen des industriellen Bambusbodens, den gelben Stühlen im Esszimmer und den rosafarbenen Vorhängen bildet, die die Atmosphäre auflockern. Die Küche ist in einem kräftigen Blau gehalten und kombiniert geometrische Muster, die an die Frische des Mittelmeers erinnern, während natürliche Holzdetails das Ganze abmildern. Der Waschraum für die Jugendlichen ist eine Explosion von Gelb, während das Hauptbadezimmer durch tiefe Blautöne und Holzdetails gekennzeichnet ist. Der Zugang zum Hauptschlafzimmer ist mit einer Vertäfelung in einem tiefen, warmen Rosa versehen, die ein Gefühl von Gemütlichkeit und Ruhe vermittelt.

La surprise attend dans chaque recoin de cette maison, où le design transcende le fonctionnel pour devenir une expérience sensorielle. Ici, la couleur n'est pas un simple complément, mais le fil conducteur d'une atmosphère vibrante et dynamique. Le nouvel agencement, fruit d'une rénovation, privilégie l'espace et la fluidité, supprimant les barrières visuelles pour renforcer le lien entre les espaces communs.
Le salon est mis en valeur par un pilier orange qui agit comme un point focal. Ce ton vibrant est équilibré par la sérénité d'une œuvre d'art reflétant un paysage bleu profond, créant un contraste harmonieux avec les tons chauds du sol industriel en bambou, les chaises jaunes de la salle à manger et les rideaux roses, qui adoucissent l'atmosphère. La cuisine, audacieuse dans sa couleur bleu profond, combine des motifs géométriques qui évoquent la fraîcheur de la Méditerranée, tandis que des détails en bois naturel adoucissent l'ensemble. La salle de bains des adolescents est une explosion de jaune, tandis que la salle de bains principale est identifiée par des tons bleus profonds et des détails en bois. L'accès à la chambre principale est marqué par un lambris d'un rose profond et chaud qui donne une impression de confort et de calme.

La sorpresa aguarda en cada rincón de esta vivienda, donde el diseño trasciende lo funcional para convertirse en una experiencia sensorial. Aquí, el color no es un simple complemento, sino el hilo conductor de una atmósfera vibrante y dinámica. La nueva distribución resultante de una reforma, apuesta por la amplitud y la fluidez, derribando barreras visuales para potenciar la conexión entre los espacios comunes.
El salón destaca por un pilar naranja que actúa como punto focal. Este vibrante tono se equilibra con la serenidad de una obra de arte que refleja un paisaje azul profundo, creando un contraste armonioso con los cálidos tonos del suelo de bambú industrial, las sillas amarillas del comedor y las cortinas rosas, que suavizan el ambiente. La cocina, audaz en su color azul intenso, combina patrones geométricos que evocan la frescura del Mediterráneo, mientras que los detalles en madera natural suavizan el conjunto. El aseo de los adolescentes es una explosión de amarillo, mientras que el baño principal se identifica con tonos azules profundos y detalles en madera. El acceso al dormitorio principal, está marcado por panelados en un rosa intenso y cálido que transmite una sensación de acogida e induce a la calma.

EL OJO

In this house, color is not just a complement but the thread that weaves a vibrant and dynamic atmosphere.

CONSTANZE LADNER

THE FIG TREE HOUSE >

MAINZ, GERMANY

Photos: © Robert Rieger

THE FIG TREE HOUSE

Color is the guiding thread in the transformation of an old rectory. This 1967 home, with its outdated aesthetic of reddish bricks, aged linoleum, and low ceilings, needed a new identity. Inspired by the lush garden and its majestic fig tree, the designer conceived a color concept that harmonizes with the existing architecture, filling the spaces with warmth and character.
Each room is defined by a specific palette. In the study, the deep green of the fig tree covers the walls and cabinets, complemented by a vibrant sun-yellow accent on a velvet sofa. The kitchen and dining area feature a bold spectrum of burgundy and deep red, softened by lighter tones on the walls and ceilings. Ladner did not hesitate to incorporate textiles into the kitchen, creating a welcoming atmosphere with sheer curtains and custom wooden furniture. The use of tone-on-tone colors, combined with textures such as velvet, plush rugs, and natural wood, adds balance and depth. In every corner, the designer achieves a dialogue between interior and exterior, where vibrant hues and the surrounding tranquility coexist in perfect harmony.

Farbe ist das zentrale Element bei der Transformation eines ehemaligen Pfarrhauses. Das 1967 erbaute Gebäude mit seiner veralteten Ästhetik aus rötlichem Backstein, gealtertem Linoleum und niedrigen Decken brauchte eine neue Identität. Inspiriert von der Üppigkeit des Gartens und seinem majestätischen Feigenbaum, entwickelte die Designerin ein Farbkonzept, das mit der bestehenden Architektur harmoniert und den Räumen Wärme und Charakter verleiht.
Jeder Raum hat eine eigene Farbpalette: Im Arbeitszimmer dominieren tiefes Feigenbaumgrün an Wänden und Schränken sowie ein lebendiges Sonnengelb, das sich auf dem Samtsofa hervorhebt. Küche und Essbereich präsentieren ein mutiges Spektrum von Burgunderrot bis tiefem Rot, das durch sanftere Wand- und Deckenfarben ausgeglichen wird. Ladner scheute sich nicht, auch in der Küche Textilien zu verwenden, um mit leichten Vorhängen und maßgefertigten Holzmöbeln eine gemütliche Atmosphäre zu schaffen. Das Spiel mit Ton-in-Ton-Farben, kombiniert mit Samt, weichen Teppichen und natürlichem Holz, verleiht den Räumen Balance und Tiefe. In jedem Winkel schafft die Designerin einen Dialog zwischen Innen- und Außenraum, in dem lebendige Nuancen und die Ruhe der Umgebung perfekt harmonieren.

La couleur est le fil conducteur de la transformation d'un ancien presbytère. La maison de 1967, avec son esthétique désuète de briques rougeâtres, de linoléum vieilli et de plafonds bas, avait besoin d'une nouvelle identité. Inspiré par la luxuriance du jardin et son figuier majestueux, le designer a conçu un concept de couleurs qui s'harmonise avec l'architecture existante, en remplissant les espaces de chaleur et de caractère.
Chaque pièce est définie par une palette spécifique. Dans le bureau, le vert intense du figuier recouvre les murs et les armoires, en harmonie avec un jaune soleil vibrant qui se détache sur le canapé en velours. La cuisine et la salle à manger présentent une gamme audacieuse de bordeaux et de rouges profonds, adoucis par des tons plus clairs sur les murs et les plafonds. Ladner n'a pas hésité à incorporer des textiles dans la cuisine pour créer une atmosphère chaleureuse avec des rideaux légers et des meubles en bois sur mesure. L'utilisation de couleurs ton sur ton, associées à des textures telles que le velours, les tapis moelleux et le bois naturel, apporte équilibre et profondeur. Dans tous les coins, le designer réussit à créer un dialogue entre l'intérieur et l'extérieur, où les teintes vibrantes et la sérénité de l'environnement coexistent en parfaite harmonie.

El color es el hilo conductor en la transformación de un antiguo rectorado. La vivienda de 1967, con su estética desactualizada de ladrillos rojizos, linóleo envejecido y techos bajos, necesitaba una nueva identidad. Inspirada en la exuberancia del jardín y su majestuosa higuera, la diseñadora concibió un concepto cromático que armoniza con la arquitectura existente, llenando los espacios de calidez y carácter.
Cada estancia se define por una paleta específica. En el estudio, el verde intenso de la higuera cubre paredes y armarios, en sintonía con un vibrante amarillo sol que resalta sobre el sofá de terciopelo. La cocina y el comedor despliegan una audaz gama de borgoña y rojo profundo, suavizados por tonos más claros en paredes y techos. Ladner no dudó en incorporar textiles en la cocina para crear una atmósfera acogedora con cortinas ligeras y mobiliario de madera a medida. El uso de colores tono sobre tono, combinado con texturas como terciopelo, alfombras mullidas y madera natural, aporta equilibrio y profundidad. En cada rincón, la diseñadora logra un diálogo entre interior y exterior, donde los matices vibrantes y la serenidad del entorno conviven en perfecta armonía.

Inspired by the garden and fig tree,
the designer's color concept enhances the
architecture with warmth and character.

PASSAGEN

CRAIE CRAIE

JACQUARD >

LYON, FRANCE
Photos: © Sabine Serrad

JACQUARD

Located in the bohemian district of Croix-Rousse in Lyon, this flat belongs to a young couple who wanted to update an outdated space. True to their style, CRAIE CRAIE carried out a renovation defined by vibrant colours and dynamic volumes. The living room was transformed into the heart of the home, with a revamped parquet floor and a blue bookshelf on either side of the fireplace, which takes all the attention. The space was divided into two parts: on one side, a glass wall created a new room, ideal for use as an office or guest room; and on the other, a cosy dining room, delimited by a wall with an open arch. In the hallway, the black and white checkerboard tiles were retained and the ceiling was painted sky blue to soften the verticality. In the kitchen, every centimetre was optimised with custom-made furniture, and the emerald green colour contrasts with coloured shelves. The boiler is hidden behind a rounded Memphis-style cabinet, and iridescent mosaic tiling completes the design. In the bedroom, a Klein blue wall contrasts with pink cupboards, while terracotta and rattan doors add lightness. The bathroom, renovated with teal tiles and fuchsia grouting, adds freshness to the ensemble.

Diese Wohnung im Bohème-Viertel Croix-Rousse in Lyon gehört einem jungen Paar, das einen veralteten Raum modernisieren wollte. CRAIE CRAIE hat eine Renovierung durchgeführt, die sich durch lebendige Farben und dynamische Volumen auszeichnet. Das Wohnzimmer wurde in das Herz der Wohnung verwandelt, mit einem neu gestalteten Parkettboden und einem blauen Bücherregal zu beiden Seiten des Kamins, der die ganze Aufmerksamkeit auf sich zieht. Der Raum wurde in zwei Teile geteilt: Auf der einen Seite entstand durch eine Glaswand ein neuer Raum, der sich ideal als Büro oder Gästezimmer nutzen lässt, und auf der anderen Seite ein gemütliches Esszimmer, das durch eine Wand mit offenem Bogen begrenzt wird. Im Korridor wurden die schwarz-weißen Schachbrettfliesen beibehalten und die Decke himmelblau gestrichen, um die Vertikalität abzumildern. In der Küche wurde jeder Zentimeter mit maßgefertigten Möbeln optimiert. Der Boiler ist hinter einem abgerundeten Schrank im Memphis-Stil versteckt, und schillernde Mosaikfliesen vervollständigen das Design. Im Schlafzimmer kontrastiert eine kleinblaue Wand mit rosafarbenen Schränken, während Terrakotta- und Rattantüren für Leichtigkeit sorgen. Das Badezimmer, das mit tealfarbenen Fliesen und fuchsiafarbenen Fugen renoviert wurde, bringt Frische in das Ensemble.

Situé dans le quartier bohème de la Croix-Rousse à Lyon, cet appartement appartient à un jeune couple qui souhaitait remettre au goût du jour un espace désuet. Fidèle à leur style, CRAIE CRAIE a réalisé une rénovation marquée par des couleurs vives et des volumes dynamiques. Le salon est devenu le cœur de la maison, avec un parquet revisité et une bibliothèque bleue de part et d'autre de la cheminée, qui attire tous les regards. L'espace a été divisé en deux parties : d'un côté, une paroi vitrée crée une nouvelle pièce, idéale pour servir de bureau ou de chambre d'amis ; de l'autre, une salle à manger accueillante, délimitée par un mur avec une arche ouverte. Dans le couloir, le carrelage en damier noir et blanc a été conservé et le plafond a été peint en bleu ciel pour adoucir la verticalité. Dans la cuisine, chaque centimètre a été optimisé avec du mobilier sur mesure et la couleur vert émeraude contraste avec les étagères colorées. La chaudière est cachée derrière un meuble arrondi de style Memphis, et un carrelage en mosaïque irisée complète l'aménagement. Dans la chambre, un mur bleu Klein contraste avec des placards roses, tandis que des portes en terre cuite et en rotin apportent de la légèreté. Dans la salle de bain, la rénovation avec des carreaux bleu-vert et des joints fuchsia apporte de la fraîcheur à l'ensemble.

Situado en el barrio bohemio de Croix-Rousse en Lyon, este apartamento pertenece a un matrimonio joven que quería actualizar un espacio anticuado. Para ello, y fiel a su estilo, CRAIE CRAIE realizó una reforma definida por los colores vibrantes y los volúmenes dinámicos. El salón se transformó en el corazón de la vivienda, con un parquet renovado y una estantería de fondo azul a ambos lados de la chimenea, que se lleva toda la atención. El espacio se dividió en dos partes: por un lado, una pared de cristal que creó una nueva habitación, ideal para usarse como oficina o cuarto de invitados; y por el otro, un comedor acogedor, delimitado por una pared con un arco abierto. En el pasillo se conservaron los azulejos en damero blanco y negro ,y se pintó el techo de azul cielo para suavizar la verticalidad. En la cocina, se optimizó cada centímetro con muebles a medida. El color verde esmeralda contrasta con unas estanterías. La caldera se oculta tras un mueble redondeado de estilo Memphis, y el revestimiento de mosaicos iridiscentes completa el diseño. En el dormitorio, una pared azul Klein contrasta con armarios rosas, mientras que las puertas de terracota y ratán aportan ligereza. En el baño la renovación con azulejos verde azulado y juntas fucsias, aporta frescura al conjunto.

BIG MAMMA

1000 GRANDS PRIX
THE HOW
TO ISSUE

SUPREMATISM AS INSPIRATION >

KYIV, UKRAINE
Photos: © Andrey Avdeenko

SUPREMATISM AS INSPIRATION

With an identity defined by modernity, this flat embodies an aesthetic inspired by Suprematism, the artistic movement founded by Kazimir Malevich, based on abstract forms and a vibrant use of colour. The result is a contemporary interior, bathed in natural light and fully functional. Art plays a key role in the setting, with panels by artist Tasha Oro adding depth and character. One of the distinctive features is the combination of Sevesglassblock glass blocks and textured glass panels. This solution allows for clear zoning without sacrificing luminosity. In contrast, the exposed electrical wiring on the concrete introduces a subtle and sophisticated industrial nod. In the corridor, an acoustic panel made from recycled plastic bottles boldly fuses sustainability and design. Architect Yevheniia Sytnik used the RAL system for impeccable colour consistency with details such as the chair legs, washbasin and chest of drawers. Vibrant yellow tiles in the bathroom and kitchen cabinet dialogue with the graphic ceramic patterns, while floor-to-ceiling panoramic windows, clad in wooden shutters, frame breathtaking views of Kyiv.

Diese Wohnung mit ihrer von der Moderne geprägten Identität verkörpert eine Ästhetik, die vom Suprematismus inspiriert ist, der von Kasimir Malewitsch begründeten Kunstrichtung, die auf abstrakten Formen und einer lebhaften Farbgebung basiert. Das Ergebnis ist ein modernes, lichtdurchflutetes und voll funktionales Interieur. Die Kunst spielt eine wichtige Rolle in der Einrichtung, wobei die Tafeln der Künstlerin Tasha Oro Tiefe und Charakter verleihen. Eine Besonderheit ist die Kombination von Sevesglassblock-Glasbausteinen und strukturierten Glasscheiben. Diese Lösung ermöglicht eine klare Zonierung ohne Einbußen bei der Helligkeit. Im Gegensatz dazu verleihen die freiliegenden elektrischen Leitungen auf dem Beton einen subtilen und raffinierten industriellen Akzent. Im Korridor sorgt eine Akustikplatte aus recycelten Plastikflaschen für eine kühne Verbindung von Nachhaltigkeit und Design. Die Architektin Yevheniia Sytnik verwendete das RAL-System, um eine perfekte Farbkonsistenz bei Details wie Stuhlbeinen, Waschbecken und Kommode zu gewährleisten. Die leuchtend gelben Fliesen im Bad und in der Küche stehen im Dialog mit den grafischen Keramikmustern, während die raumhohen, mit Holzläden verkleideten Panoramafenster einen atemberaubenden Blick auf Kiew bieten.

Avec une identité définie par la modernité, cet appartement incarne une esthétique inspirée du suprématisme, le mouvement artistique fondé par Kazimir Malevitch, basé sur des formes abstraites et une utilisation vibrante de la couleur. Il en résulte un intérieur contemporain, baigné de lumière naturelle et entièrement fonctionnel. L'art joue un rôle clé dans le décor, avec des panneaux de l'artiste Tasha Oro qui donnent de la profondeur et du caractère à l'ensemble. L'une des caractéristiques distinctives est la combinaison de blocs de verre Sevesglassblock et de panneaux de verre texturé. Cette solution permet un zonage clair sans sacrifier la luminosité. En revanche, le câblage électrique apparent sur le béton introduit un clin d'œil industriel subtil et sophistiqué. Dans le couloir, un panneau acoustique fabriqué à partir de bouteilles en plastique recyclées fusionne audacieusement la durabilité et le design. L'architecte Yevheniia Sytnik a utilisé le système RAL pour assurer une parfaite cohérence des couleurs avec des détails tels que les pieds de chaise, le lavabo et la commode. Les carreaux jaune vif de la salle de bain et de la cuisine dialoguent avec les motifs graphiques de la céramique, tandis que les fenêtres panoramiques du sol au plafond, habillées de volets en bois, offrent une vue imprenable sur Kyiv.

Con una identidad definida por la modernidad, este apartamento encarna una estética inspirada en el Suprematismo, el movimiento artístico fundado por Kazimir Malevich, basado en formas abstractas y un uso vibrante del color. El resultado es un interior contemporáneo, bañado de luz natural y totalmente funcional. El arte juega un papel clave en la ambientación, con los paneles de la artista Tasha Oro aportando profundidad y carácter. Uno de los recursos distintivos es la combinación de bloques de vidrio de Sevesglassblock y paneles de vidrio texturizado. Esta solución permite una zonificación clara sin sacrificar luminosidad. En contraste, el cableado eléctrico expuesto sobre el hormigón introduce un guiño industrial sutil y sofisticado. En el pasillo, un panel acústico elaborado con botellas de plástico recicladas fusiona sostenibilidad y diseño de manera audaz. La arquitecta Yevheniia Sytnik recurrió al sistema RAL para una coherencia cromática impecable con detalles como las patas de las sillas, el lavabo y la cómoda. El amarillo vibrante en los azulejos del baño y el armario de cocina dialoga con los patrones gráficos cerámicos, mientras que las ventanas panorámicas de suelo a techo, vestidas con persianas de madera, enmarcan impresionantes vistas de Kyiv.

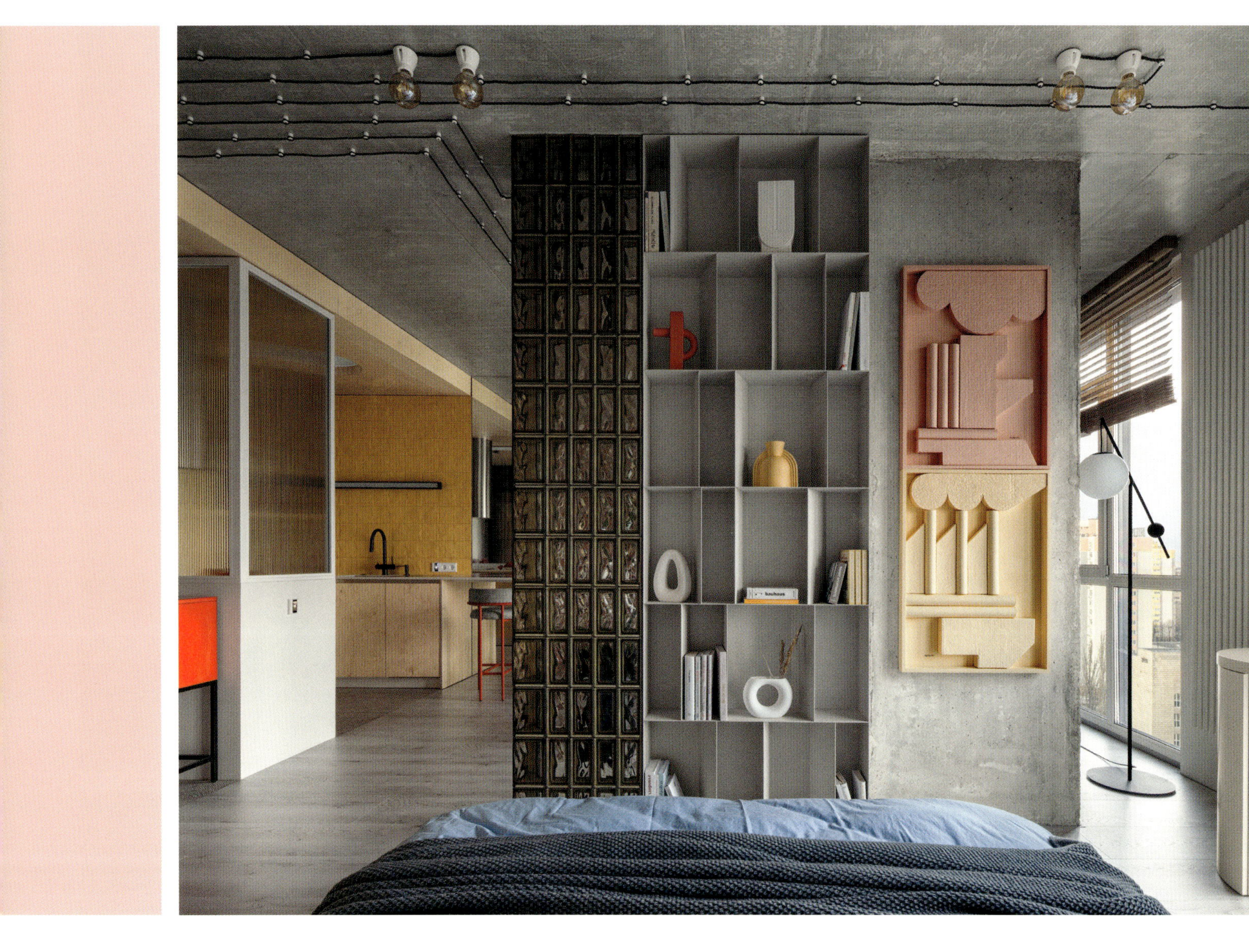

Defined by modernity, this apartment embodies an aesthetic inspired by Kazimir Malevich, based on abstract forms and a vibrant use of color.

EVEN ELEVEN
INTERIOR DESIGN STUDIO

COLOR & LIGHT IN BUSSUM >

BUSSUM, THE NETHERLANDS
Photos: © Roel Marius Brouwer

COLOR & LIGHT IN BUSSUM

Designed by Even Eleven for their own family, this home places color and pattern at the core of its identity. Here, deep purples, burnt amber, and pale yellow are combined throughout the spaces, creating a diverse visual journey—from the serene, warm terracotta pink bedroom to the dining area wrapped in a mix of deep, inviting reds.
The open-plan layout allows spaces to be connected or enclosed as needed, adapting to the dynamics of family life. A rich mix of materials—natural woods, colorful stones, glossy surfaces, and soft fabrics—adds a sense of balanced sophistication, while vintage pieces and expressive artworks reinforce the home's character. Many of these objects were collected during the family's travels, forming a personal collection that turns every corner into a visual narrative. Curved shapes, archways, and playful details contribute to a cozy and harmonious fusion of styles. The façade, featuring an aged thatched roof and charred wood, strikes a balance between traditional and contemporary elements.

Gestaltet von Even Eleven für die eigene Familie, macht dieses Haus Farbe und Muster zum zentralen Element seiner Identität. Intensive Violetttöne, verbranntes Bernstein und blasses Gelb ziehen sich durch die Räume und schaffen eine visuelle Vielfalt – vom Schlafzimmer in warmem Terrakotta-Rosa bis zum Esszimmer mit tiefroten, einladenden Nuancen.
Der offene Grundriss ermöglicht es, die Räume je nach Bedarf zu verbinden oder zu separieren, um sich an das Familienleben anzupassen. Die Vielfalt der Materialien – natürliche Hölzer, farbige Steine, glänzende Oberflächen und weiche Stoffe – verleiht dem Design eine ausgewogene Eleganz. Vintage-Stücke und ausdrucksstarke Kunstwerke unterstreichen den Charakter des Hauses. Viele dieser Objekte stammen aus Reisen der Familie und verwandeln jede Ecke in eine persönliche visuelle Erzählung. Sanfte Rundungen, Bögen und verspielte Details verstärken das Gefühl von Behaglichkeit und verbinden verschiedene Stilrichtungen harmonisch miteinander. Die Fassade mit ihrem gealterten Reetdach und verbranntem Holz schafft eine Balance zwischen traditioneller und zeitgenössischer Architektur.

Conçue par Even Eleven pour sa propre famille, cette maison fait de la couleur et des motifs l'axe central de son identité. Ici, les pourpres profonds, l'ambre brûlé et les tons jaunes pâles sont combinés dans toutes les pièces, offrant une diversité visuelle qui va de la chambre à coucher dans un rose terracotta serein et chaud à la salle à manger dans un mélange de rouges profonds et accueillants.
La conception ouverte permet de relier ou de fermer des zones en fonction des besoins de la vie familiale. La richesse des matériaux – bois naturels, pierres colorées, surfaces brillantes et tissus doux – apporte une sophistication équilibrée, tandis que les pièces vintage et les œuvres d'art choisies pour leur charge expressive renforcent le caractère de l'espace. Nombre de ces objets ont été acquis au cours de ses voyages, une collection personnelle qui transforme chaque coin en une narration visuelle. Les formes courbes, les arcs et les détails ludiques ajoutent à l'impression de confort et mélangent harmonieusement les styles. La façade, avec son toit de chaume usé par les intempéries et son bois brûlé, équilibre le traditionnel et le contemporain.

Diseñada por Even Eleven para su propia familia, esta casa convierte el color y los patrones en el eje central de su identidad. Aquí, los tonos morados intensos, ámbar quemado y amarillo pálido se combinan a lo largo de las estancias, aportando una diversidad visual que va desde el dormitorio en rosa terracota, sereno y cálido, hasta el comedor en una mezcla de rojos profundos, acogedores.
El diseño de planta abierta permite que las zonas se conecten o se cierren según sea necesario para adaptarse a la vida familiar. La riqueza de materiales —maderas naturales, piedras de colores, superficies brillantes y telas suaves— aporta una sofisticación equilibrada, mientras que las piezas vintage y las obras de arte elegidas por su carga expresiva refuerzan el carácter del espacio. Muchos de estos objetos han sido adquiridos en sus viajes, una colección personal que convierte cada rincón en un relato visual. Las formas curvas, los arcos y los detalles lúdicos suman a la sensación de confort, fusionando estilos de manera armoniosa. La fachada, con su techo de paja envejecido y la madera quemada, equilibra lo tradicional con lo contemporáneo.

AFRICAN ARTISTS

This home blends curved shapes, arches, and playful details with vibrant colors and patterns, creating a harmonious and comforting space.

Valoriani

LISA BREEZE,
ARCHITECTURE AND INTERIORS

FLEMINGTON HOUSE >

MELBOURNE, AUSTRALIA

Photos: © Catherine Schusler

FLEMINGTON HOUSE

This 1940s house, which belonged to the current owner's great aunt and uncle, was renovated with respect for its heritage but in keeping with contemporary design. The architect Lisa Breeze was inspired by the original elements, such as the terrazzo floors and the retro mint green cabinets with sliding glass doors featuring fluted patterns in the kitchen. These details guided the selection of materials and colours, creating an atmosphere that unites the classic with the modern. At the rear of the house, a small annexe was built, relocating the service areas and opening up the space to a garden. The new kitchen and dining room feature vibrant mid-century colours, with mint green cabinets as the main aesthetic element. Both spaces are visually connected to the outside, creating a bright and welcoming atmosphere. The front bedrooms and living room were renovated while maintaining their original features, with restored details that preserve the essence of the house. Every corner of the house reflects the balance between the historical preservation of what was a humble dwelling house with the needs of contemporary design, achieving a perfect harmony between the past and the present.

Dieses Haus aus den 1940er Jahren, das dem Großonkel des jetzigen Eigentümers gehörte, wurde mit Respekt vor seinem Erbe renoviert, aber an ein zeitgemäßes Design angepasst. Die Architektin Lisa Breeze ließ sich von den ursprünglichen Elementen inspirieren, wie den Terrazzo-Böden und den retro mintgrünen Schränken mit Schiebetüren aus Glas mit gerillten Mustern in der Küche. Diese Details waren ausschlaggebend für die Auswahl der Materialien und Farben und schufen eine Atmosphäre, die das Klassische mit dem Modernen verbindet. An der Rückseite des Hauses wurde ein kleiner Anbau errichtet, der die Wirtschaftsräume verlagert und den Raum zum Garten hin öffnet. Die neue Küche und das Esszimmer sind in kräftigen Mid-Century-Farben gehalten, wobei mintgrüne Schränke das wichtigste ästhetische Element sind. Beide Räume sind visuell mit dem Außenbereich verbunden und schaffen eine helle und einladende Atmosphäre. Die vorderen Schlafzimmer und das Wohnzimmer wurden unter Beibehaltung ihrer ursprünglichen Merkmale renoviert, mit restaurierten Details, die die Essenz des Hauses bewahren. Jeder Winkel des Hauses spiegelt das Gleichgewicht zwischen der historischen Erhaltung eines bescheidenen Wohnhauses und den Anforderungen an ein zeitgemäßes Design wider, wodurch eine perfekte Harmonie zwischen der Vergangenheit und der Gegenwart erreicht wird.

Cette maison des années 1940, qui appartenait au grand-oncle de l'actuelle propriétaire, a été rénovée dans le respect de son patrimoine, tout en l'adaptant au design contemporain. L'architecte Lisa Breeze s'est inspirée des éléments originaux, tels que les sols en terrazzo et les armoires rétro vert menthe avec des portes coulissantes en verre à motifs cannelés dans la cuisine. Ces détails ont guidé le choix des matériaux et des couleurs, créant une atmosphère qui allie le classique et le moderne. À l'arrière de la maison, une petite annexe a été construite, déplaçant les zones de service et ouvrant l'espace sur un jardin. La nouvelle cuisine et la salle à manger arborent des couleurs vives du milieu du siècle, avec des armoires vert menthe comme principal élément esthétique. Les deux espaces sont visuellement reliés à l'extérieur, créant une atmosphère lumineuse et accueillante. Les chambres et le salon situés à l'avant ont été rénovés tout en conservant leurs caractéristiques d'origine, avec des détails restaurés qui préservent l'essence de la maison. Chaque recoin de la maison reflète l'équilibre entre la préservation historique de ce qui était une humble maison d'habitation et les besoins du design contemporain, réalisant ainsi une harmonie parfaite entre le passé et le présent.

Esta casa de la década de 1940, que perteneció a los tíos abuelos del actual propietario, fue renovada respetando su herencia, pero adaptándola al diseño contemporáneo. La arquitecta Lisa Breeze se inspiró en los elementos originales, como los suelos de terrazo y los armarios retro en color verde menta con puertas correderas en cristal ranurado en la cocina. Estos detalles guiaron la selección de materiales y colores, creando una atmósfera que une lo clásico con lo moderno. En la parte trasera de la casa se construyó un pequeño anexo, reubicando las áreas de servicio y abriendo el espacio hacia un jardín. La nueva cocina y el comedor, destacan por los colores vibrantes de mediados de siglo, con los armarios verde menta como principal elemento estético. Ambos espacios se conectan visualmente con el exterior, creando un ambiente luminoso y acogedor. Los dormitorios frontales y la sala de estar se renovaron manteniendo sus características originales, con detalles restaurados que preservan la esencia de la casa. Cada rincón de la casa refleja el equilibrio entre la preservación histórica de lo que era una humilde vivienda casa con las necesidades del diseño contemporáneo, logrando una armonía perfecta entre el pasado y el presente.

The house balances historical preservation with contemporary design, harmonizing the past and present.

SLOANE COURT WEST APARTMENT >

LONDON, UNITED KINGDOM

Photos: © Matt Clayton

SLOANE COURT WEST APARTMENT

Colour plays a central role in the renovation of this Sloane Square duplex, where every space has been conceived to highlight vibrant hues and expressive materials. From the ceramic fireplace in the living room to the burgundy-stained carved wood shelving, the intervention balances chromatic boldness and spatial harmony. The ground floor was transformed into a fluid area integrating kitchen, dining room and living room. One of the main challenges was to design a kitchen that broke with conventional aesthetics, resolving it with an asymmetrical island and floating shelves to display decorative ceramics. A key element in the layout is the system of folding doors intervened by the artist Tuesday Riddle, whose illustrations evoke the cultural heritage of the owners. On the lower floor, the reorganisation allowed for the addition of two en-suite bedrooms, connected by a curved staircase. Gold-toned stucco and a custom light fixture designed by Margit Wittig emphasise the verticality of the space. In the master bedroom, a soft palette enriches the connection with the outdoor courtyard, where a green wall brings greenery inside. In the second bedroom, dynamic wallpaper dialogues with a matching upholstered headboard.

Farbe spielt eine zentrale Rolle bei der Renovierung dieses Doppelhauses am Sloane Square, wo jeder Raum so konzipiert wurde, dass lebendige Farbtöne und ausdrucksstarke Materialien im Vordergrund stehen. Vom keramischen Kamin im Wohnzimmer bis hin zu den geschnitzten, burgunderrot gebeizten Bücherregalen wurde ein Gleichgewicht zwischen chromatischer Kühnheit und räumlicher Harmonie geschaffen. Das Erdgeschoss wurde in einen fließenden Bereich verwandelt, der Küche, Esszimmer und Wohnzimmer miteinander verbindet. Eine der größten Herausforderungen bestand darin, eine Küche zu entwerfen, die mit der konventionellen Ästhetik bricht, was mit einer asymmetrischen Insel und schwebenden Regalen zur Präsentation dekorativer Keramik gelöst wurde. Ein Schlüsselelement der Einrichtung ist das System der Falttüren, das von der Künstlerin Tuesday Riddle gestaltet wurde und dessen Illustrationen an das kulturelle Erbe der Eigentümer erinnern. Im unteren Stockwerk konnten durch die Umgestaltung zwei Schlafzimmer mit eigenem Bad eingerichtet werden, die durch eine geschwungene Treppe verbunden sind. Der goldene Stuck und eine maßgefertigte Leuchte, entworfen von Margit Witting, betonen die Vertikalität des Raums. Im Hauptschlafzimmer wird durch eine sanfte Farbgebung die Verbindung zum Innenhof hergestellt, wo eine grüne Wand das Grün ins Haus holt. Im zweiten Schlafzimmer steht eine dynamische Tapete im Dialog mit einem passenden gepolsterten Kopfteil.

La couleur joue un rôle central dans la rénovation de ce duplex de Sloane Square, où chaque espace a été conçu pour mettre en valeur des teintes vibrantes et des matériaux expressifs. De la cheminée en céramique du salon aux bibliothèques en bois sculpté teinté en bordeaux, l'intervention équilibre audace chromatique et harmonie spatiale. Le rez-de-chaussée a été transformé en un espace fluide intégrant la cuisine, la salle à manger et le salon. L'un des principaux défis consistait à concevoir une cuisine qui rompait avec l'esthétique conventionnelle, en la résolvant avec un îlot asymétrique et des étagères flottantes pour exposer des céramiques décoratives. Un élément clé de l'aménagement est le système de portes pliantes réalisé par l'artiste Tuesday Riddle, dont les illustrations évoquent l'héritage culturel des propriétaires. À l'étage inférieur, la réorganisation a permis d'ajouter deux chambres avec salle de bains, reliées par un escalier incurvé. Le stuc doré et un luminaire designée par Margit Witting sur mesure soulignent la verticalité de l'espace. Dans la chambre principale, une palette douce enrichit le lien avec la cour extérieure, où un mur vert apporte de la verdure à l'intérieur. Dans la deuxième chambre, un papier peint dynamique dialogue avec une tête de lit rembourrée assortie.

El color juega un papel central en la reforma de este dúplex en Sloane Square, donde cada espacio ha sido concebido para resaltar tonalidades vibrantes y materiales expresivos. Desde la chimenea de cerámica en la sala de estar hasta las estanterías en madera tallada teñida en burdeos, la intervención equilibra audacia cromática y armonía espacial. La planta baja se transformó en un área fluida que integra cocina, comedor y sala de estar. Uno de los principales retos fue diseñar una cocina que rompiera con la estética convencional, resolviéndose con una isla asimétrica y estantes flotantes para exhibir cerámicas decorativas. Un elemento clave en la distribución es el sistema de puertas plegables intervenidas por la artista Tuesday Riddle, cuyas ilustraciones evocan el legado cultural de los propietarios. En la planta inferior, la reorganización permitió incorporar dos dormitorios en suite, conectados por una escalera curva. El estuco en tonos dorados y una luminaria a medida diseñada por Margit Wittig enfatizan la verticalidad del espacio. En el dormitorio principal, una paleta suave enriquece la conexión con el patio exterior, donde un muro verde introduce vegetación en el interior. En el segundo dormitorio, un papel pintado dinámico dialoga con un cabecero tapizado a juego.

LongHouse
HAMPTONS PRIVATE

A versatile lounge where a wood and plexiglass bookcase frames a striking stained-glass St. Christopher, while bold, patterned upholstery infuses the space with vibrancy.

Das Brandenburger Tor
PICASSO
CABINS

LUCIE SOCRATE STUDIO

APPARTEMENT MERVEILLEUX >

ENGHIEN-LES-BAINS, FRANCE
Photos: © Herve Goluza

APPARTEMENT MERVEILLEUX

Inspired by the vibrant city of Rio de Janeiro, the renovation of this 60 m² flat combines chromatic boldness, functional design and subtle references to the 1960s and 1970s, while preserving the classic elements of Parisian interior design.
The colour palette plays with contrasts between warm tones - ochre, red brown and wood - and cool tones - sky blue, green and grey - evoking the energy of Ipanema beach. The furniture, expressly selected to achieve a vintage feel, adds personality, while the Scandinavian pieces in dark wood establish a dialogue with Brazilian design, subtly reinterpreted. The Plum.Living kitchen becomes the heart of the setting, with its play of contrasts and clean lines. The omnipresent vegetation pays homage to the Jardim Botânico carioca, integrating nature into everyday life. The design balances masculine and feminine codes, combining soft shapes and cheerful colours with more sober elements. Sustainability has guided every choice, from the intelligent redistribution of spaces to the choice of recycled materials and committed suppliers.

Inspiriert von der pulsierenden Stadt Rio de Janeiro, kombiniert die Renovierung dieser 60 m² großen Wohnung chromatische Kühnheit, funktionelles Design und subtile Anspielungen auf die 1960er und 1970er Jahre, wobei die klassischen Elemente der Pariser Innenarchitektur erhalten bleiben.
Die Farbpalette spielt mit Kontrasten zwischen warmen Tönen - Ocker, Rotbraun und Holz - und kühlen Tönen - Himmelblau, Grün und Grau - und erinnert an die Energie des Strandes von Ipanema. Die eigens für den Vintage-Stil ausgewählten Möbel verleihen Persönlichkeit, während die skandinavischen Möbel aus dunklem Holz einen Dialog mit dem brasilianischen Design aufnehmen, das auf subtile Weise neu interpretiert wird. Die Küche von Plum.Living wird mit ihrem Spiel mit Kontrasten und klaren Linien zum Herzstück der Einrichtung. Die allgegenwärtige Vegetation ist eine Hommage an den Jardim Botânico Carioca und integriert die Natur in das tägliche Leben. Das Design schafft ein Gleichgewicht zwischen maskulinen und femininen Codes und kombiniert weiche Formen und fröhliche Farben mit nüchternen Elementen. Bei jeder Entscheidung wurde auf Nachhaltigkeit geachtet, von der intelligenten Neuaufteilung der Räume bis hin zur Auswahl von recycelten Materialien und engagierten Lieferanten.

Inspirée par l'effervescence de Rio de Janeiro, la rénovation de cet appartement de 60 m² allie audace chromatique, design fonctionnel et références subtiles aux années 1960 et 1970, tout en préservant les éléments classiques de l'architecture d'intérieur parisienne.
La palette de couleurs joue sur les contrastes entre les tons chauds — ocre, brun rouge et bois — et les tons froids — bleu ciel, vert et gris — évoquant l'énergie de la plage d'Ipanema. Le mobilier, expressément sélectionné pour obtenir un effet vintage, apporte de la personnalité, tandis que les pièces scandinaves en bois sombre établissent un dialogue avec le design brésilien, subtilement réinterprété. La cuisine Plum.Living devient le cœur du décor, avec son jeu de contrastes et ses lignes épurées. La végétation omniprésente rend hommage au Jardim Botânico carioca, intégrant la nature au quotidien. Le design équilibre les codes masculins et féminins, combinant des formes douces et des couleurs gaies avec des éléments plus sobres. La durabilité a guidé tous les choix, de la redistribution intelligente des espaces au choix de matériaux recyclés et de fournisseurs engagés.

Inspirado en la vibrante ciudad de Río de Janeiro, la renovación de este apartamento de 60 m² combina audacia cromática, diseño funcional y referencias sutiles a los años 60 y 70, preservando a la vez los elementos clásicos del interiorismo parisino.
La paleta de colores juega con contrastes entre tonos cálidos —ocre, rojo marrón y madera— y fríos —azul cielo, verde y gris—, evocando la energía de la playa de Ipanema. El mobiliario expresamente seleccionado para conseguir un aire vintage, aporta personalidad, mientras que las piezas escandinavas de madera oscura establecen un diálogo con el diseño brasileño, reinterpretado con sutileza.La cocina de de Plum.Living se convierte en el corazón de la escenografía, con sus juegos de contraste y líneas depuradas. La vegetación omnipresente rinde homenaje al Jardim Botânico carioca, integrando la naturaleza en la vida cotidiana. El diseño equilibra códigos masculinos y femeninos, combinando formas suaves y colores alegres con elementos más sobrios. La sostenibilidad ha guiado cada elección, desde la redistribución inteligente de los espacios hasta la elección de materiales reciclados y proveedores comprometidos.

Inspired by the vibrant city of Rio de Janeiro, this apartment renovation showcases bold colors, functional design, and subtle nods to the '60s and '70s.

MARTÍN PELÁEZ ESTUDIO

NEDU >

MADRID, SPAIN

Photos: © Alberto Amores

NEDU

Color guides the transformation of this home, located in a building from 1882 in Plaza Mayor. Its location in a bustling city center contrasts with the serene atmosphere of its interior, where five windows frame the sky in its constant variations of light and hue. The client, with a joyful and sociable spirit, desired a vibrant, immersive home with a strong identity. To achieve this, the design was structured around four key elements: color, geometry, materiality, and visual continuity. The original pillars and beams were restored, previously isolated spaces were integrated, and the available height was maximized. The color palette evokes the sky—deep blues, iridescent reflections, sunset oranges, and lilacs. These appear in furniture, storage, and wall coverings. Curved shapes, inspired by clouds, are reflected in the central table, which wraps around a pillar and seems to float. Light, a key element in the project, is amplified by reflective surfaces and strategic shadow play. The materials reinforce the concept: gray floors, white walls, and tiles in twilight tones. Finally, two paintings by Candela Picado de Blas add a playful touch, completing this interpretation of the sky of Madrid.

Farbe führt die Transformation dieses Wohnraums in einem Gebäude von 1882 auf der Plaza Mayor an. Seine Lage in einer belebten Umgebung steht im Kontrast zur ruhigen Atmosphäre des Innenraums, in dem fünf Fenster den Himmel in seinen ständigen Licht- und Farbveränderungen einrahmen. Der Auftraggeber, ein fröhlicher und geselliger Mensch, wünschte sich ein lebendiges, einhüllendes Zuhause mit starker Identität. Um dies zu erreichen, wurde das Design um vier Achsen herum strukturiert: Farbe, Geometrie, Materialität und visuelle Kontinuität. Die originalen Säulen und Balken wurden restauriert, zuvor isolierte Räume integriert und die vorhandene Höhe maximiert. Die Farbpalette erinnert an den Himmel: intensive Blautöne, irisierende Reflexe, Orangetöne und fliederfarbene Nuancen des Sonnenuntergangs. Diese finden sich in Möbeln, Stauraumlösungen und Wandverkleidungen wieder. Geschwungene Formen, inspiriert von Wolken, spiegeln sich im zentralen Tisch wider, der eine Säule umgibt und zu schweben scheint. Licht ist ein Schlüsselelement des Projekts und wird durch reflektierende Oberflächen und strategische Schattenspiele verstärkt. Materialien unterstützen das Konzept: graue Böden, weiße Wände und Mosaike in dämmernden Farbtönen. Zwei Gemälde von Candela Picado de Blas bringen eine spielerische Note ein und vervollständigen diese Interpretation des Himmels im Madrids.

La couleur guide la transformation de cette maison située dans un bâtiment datant de 1882 sur la Plaza Mayor. Sa situation dans un centre-ville animé contraste avec l'atmosphère sereine de son intérieur, où cinq fenêtres encadrent le ciel dans ses variations constantes de lumière et de tonalité. Le client, à l'esprit joyeux et sociable, souhaitait une maison vibrante, enveloppante et dotée d'une forte identité. Pour ce faire, la conception s'est articulée autour de quatre axes : la couleur, la géométrie, la matérialité et la continuité visuelle. Les piliers et les poutres d'origine ont été récupérés, les espaces précédemment isolés ont été intégrés et la hauteur disponible a été maximisée. La palette de couleurs évoque le ciel : bleus intenses, reflets irisés, oranges et lilas du couchant. Elle se retrouve dans le mobilier, les rangements et les revêtements. Les formes courbes, inspirées des nuages, se reflètent dans la table centrale, qui s'enroule autour d'un pilier et semble flotter. La lumière, élément clé du projet, est amplifiée par des surfaces réfléchissantes et des jeux d'ombres stratégiques. Les matériaux renforcent le concept : sols gris, murs blancs et mosaïques dans des tons crépusculaires. Enfin, deux peintures de Candela Picado de Blas ajoutent une touche ludique, clôturant cette interprétation du ciel de Madrid.

El color guía la transformación de esta vivienda situada en un edificio del año 1882 en la Plaza Mayor. Su ubicación en un entorno bullicioso del centro contrasta con la atmósfera serena de su interior, donde cinco ventanas enmarcan el cielo en sus constantes variaciones de luz y tonalidad. El cliente, de espíritu alegre y sociable, deseaba un hogar vibrante, envolvente y con una fuerte identidad. Para lograrlo, el diseño se estructuró en torno a cuatro ejes: color, geometría, materialidad y continuidad visual. Se recuperaron los pilares y vigas originales, se integraron espacios antes aislados y se potenció la altura disponible.La paleta cromática evoca el cielo: azules intensos, reflejos irisados, naranjas y lilas de atardecer. Aparece en muebles, almacenaje y revestimientos. Las formas curvas, inspiradas en nubes, se reflejan en la mesa central, que envuelve un pilar y parece flotar. La luz, clave en el proyecto, se amplifica con superficies reflectantes y estratégicos juegos de sombras. Los materiales refuerzan el concepto: suelos grises, paredes blancas y mosaicos en tonos crepusculares. Finalmente, dos pinturas de Candela Picado de Blas aportan un punto lúdico, cerrando esta interpretación del cielo de Madrid.

The sky-inspired color palette of blues, iridescent hues, and sunset tones defines this apartment in central Madrid.

CASA COA >

SAN MIGUEL DE ALLENDE, MEXICO
Photos: © Leandro Bulzzano

SIN TI

CASA COA

Located on one of the most emblematic streets of San Miguel de Allende, Casa Coa is a residential proposal that fuses Mexico's rich colonial history with contemporary elements in an eclectic architectural design. The 600 m^2 house is distributed over two floors connected by central courtyards, which generate a fluid transition between spaces.
The design is inspired by colonial architecture, fusing traditional arches with contemporary elements to create a warm and seductive atmosphere. The palette of green tones is harmoniously interwoven with touches of red, pink and burgundy, creating a vibrant and welcoming atmosphere, a chromatic approach inspired by nature and a romantic aesthetic. Materials used include handcrafted tiles from Dolores Hidalgo and clay and terracotta finishes that complement the historic setting. The snake-shaped door handles, made of blacksmithing, are one of the distinctive details that add a fun touch. The integration of Mexican art and culture enriches the home, with pieces by Latin American artists adding authenticity to the ambience.

Das Casa Coa liegt in einer der emblematischsten Straßen von San Miguel de Allende und ist ein Wohnprojekt, das die reiche Kolonialgeschichte Mexikos mit zeitgenössischen Elementen in einem eklektischen architektonischen Design verbindet. Das 600 m^2 große Haus ist auf zwei Etagen verteilt, die durch zentrale Innenhöfe miteinander verbunden sind, die einen fließenden Übergang zwischen den Räumen schaffen.
Das Design ist von der Kolonialarchitektur inspiriert und verbindet traditionelle Bögen mit zeitgenössischen Elementen, um eine warme und verführerische Atmosphäre zu schaffen. Die Palette der Grüntöne ist harmonisch mit Rot-, Rosa- und Burgundertönen verwoben und schafft so eine lebendige und einladende Atmosphäre, eine von der Natur inspirierte Farbgebung und eine romantische Ästhetik. Zu den verwendeten Materialien gehören handgefertigte Fliesen aus Dolores Hidalgo und Oberflächen aus Ton und Terrakotta, die das historische Ambiente ergänzen. Die schlangenförmigen Türgriffe aus Schmiedeeisen sind eines der charakteristischen Details, die dem Haus eine lustige Note verleihen. Die Integration mexikanischer Kunst und Kultur bereichert das Haus, wobei die Werke lateinamerikanischer Künstler dem Ambiente Authentizität verleihen.

Située dans l'une des rues les plus emblématiques de San Miguel de Allende, la Casa Coa est une proposition résidentielle qui fusionne la riche histoire coloniale du Mexique avec des éléments contemporains dans une conception architecturale éclectique. La maison de 600 m^2 est répartie sur deux étages reliés par des cours centrales qui créent une transition fluide entre les espaces.
Le design s'inspire de l'architecture coloniale, fusionnant les arches traditionnelles avec des éléments contemporains pour créer une atmosphère chaleureuse et séduisante. La palette de tons verts est harmonieusement entrelacée avec des touches de rouge, de rose et de bordeaux, créant une atmosphère vibrante et accueillante, une approche chromatique inspirée par la nature et une esthétique romantique. Les matériaux utilisés comprennent des carreaux artisanaux de Dolores Hidalgo et des finitions en argile et en terre cuite qui complètent le cadre historique. Les poignées de porte en forme de serpent, réalisées en forge, sont l'un des détails distinctifs qui ajoutent une touche amusante. L'intégration de l'art et de la culture mexicains enrichit la maison, avec des pièces d'artistes latino-américains qui ajoutent de l'authenticité à l'ambiance.

Ubicada en una de las calles más emblemáticas de San Miguel de Allende, Casa Coa es una propuesta residencial que fusiona la rica historia colonial de México con elementos contemporáneos en un diseño arquitectónico ecléctico. La casa de 600 m^2, se distribuye en dos plantas conectadas por patios centrales, que generan una transición fluida entre los espacios.
El diseño se inspira en la arquitectura colonial, fusionando arcos tradicionales con elementos contemporáneos para crear un ambiente cálido y seductor. La paleta de tonalidades verdes se entrelaza armoniosamente con toques de rojo, rosa y borgoña, creando una atmósfera vibrante y acogedora, un enfoque cromático inspirado en la naturaleza y una estética romántica. Entre los materiales utilizados aparecen azulejos artesanales de Dolores Hidalgo y acabados de arcilla y terracota que complementan el entorno histórico. Las manillas en las puertas con forma de serpiente y fabricadas en herrería, son uno de los detalles distintivos que añaden un toque divertido. La integración de arte y cultura mexicana enriquece el hogar, con piezas de artistas latinoamericanos que aportan autenticidad al ambiente.

The design blends colonial architecture with contemporary elements, featuring a warm atmosphere and a warm palette.

MIRTA OTTAVIANI

LA TORRE >

APULIA, ITALY

Photos: © Mirko Morelli

LA TORRE

Apulia, in southern Italy, is a region known for its olive groves and vernacular architecture. There, along the Adriatic Sea, stands this villa—initially austere and lacking personality—that was completely transformed while respecting local traditions. For the renovation, architect Mirta Ottaviani focused on using native materials such as limestone, wood, and lime. The flooring, made of hand-laid limestone, creates a warm atmosphere. The walls, coated with natural plaster and lime-painted, take on a golden hue reminiscent of the historic palazzos of Lecce. The L-shaped layout of the house opens to the garden through large windows that allow light to flood the interiors. The porch, with its gentle arches, is the heart of the home. Color plays a key role. Inside, bold tones such as red, green, and yellow appear mainly in textiles and curtains, but also in furniture and decorative details. Outside, green windows and a Greek-style baseboard reinforce the house's personality. The white facades are enriched by the green of the frames and baseboards, while terracotta details—such as downspouts and lanterns—add warmth and authenticity.

Apulien im Süden Italiens ist bekannt für seine Olivenhaine und seine traditionelle Architektur. Dort, am Ufer der Adria, befindet sich diese einst schlichte und charakterlose Villa, die komplett umgestaltet wurde, wobei die lokalen Traditionen respektiert blieben. Für die Renovierung setzte die Architektin Mirta Ottaviani auf einheimische Materialien wie Kalkstein, Holz und Kalk. Der Boden, aus handverlegtem Kalkstein gefertigt, schafft eine warme Atmosphäre. Die Wände, mit Naturputz beschichtet und mit Kalkfarbe gestrichen, nehmen einen goldenen Ton an, der an die Fassaden der historischen Paläste von Lecce erinnert. Der Grundriss in L-Form öffnet sich zum Garten hin durch große Fenster, die Licht in die Räume strömen lassen. Die Veranda mit ihren sanften Rundbögen bildet das Herz des Hauses. Farbe spielt eine zentrale Rolle. Im Inneren wurden starke Töne wie Rot, Grün und Gelb verwendet, hauptsächlich in Stoffen und Vorhängen, aber auch in Möbeln und dekorativen Details. Außen verstärken grüne Fenster und ein griechischer Sockel den Charakter des Hauses. Die weißen Fassaden harmonieren mit den grünen Rahmen und Sockeln, während Terrakottadetails, wie Regenrohre und Laternen, Wärme und Authentizität verleihen.

Les Pouilles, dans le sud de l'Italie, sont une région connue pour ses oliveraies et son architecture vernaculaire. C'est là, au bord de la mer Adriatique, que se trouve cette villa, initialement austère et sans personnalité, qui a été complètement transformée dans le respect des traditions locales. Pour la rénovation, l'architecte Mirta Ottaviani a misé sur l'utilisation de matériaux locaux tels que la pierre calcaire, le bois et la chaux. Le sol, en pierre calcaire posée à la main, crée une atmosphère chaleureuse. Les murs, recouverts d'un enduit naturel et peints à la chaux, prennent une teinte dorée qui rappelle les façades des demeures historiques de Lecce. Le plan en L de la maison s'ouvre sur le jardin par de grandes fenêtres qui permettent à la lumière d'inonder les espaces. Le porche, avec ses douces arches, est le cœur de la maison. La couleur joue un rôle essentiel. À l'intérieur, des tons forts de rouge, de vert et de jaune ont été utilisés, principalement dans les tissus et les rideaux, mais aussi dans le mobilier et les détails décoratifs. À l'extérieur, les fenêtres vertes et le socle grec renforcent la personnalité de la maison. Les façades blanches sont enrichies par le vert des encadrements et des plinthes, tandis que les détails en terre cuite, tels que les descentes d'eau et les lampadaires, apportent chaleur et authenticité.

Apulia, en el sur de Italia, es una región conocida por sus olivares y arquitectura vernácula. Allí, junto al mar Adriático se encuentra esta villa, inicialmente austera y sin personalidad, que fue completamente transformada, respetando las tradiciones locales. Para la reforma, la arquitecta Mirta Ottaviani se basó en el uso de materiales autóctonos como piedra caliza, madera y cal. El pavimento, realizado con piedra caliza colocada artesanalmente, crea una atmósfera cálida. Las paredes, revestidas con yeso natural y pintadas con cal, adoptan un tono dorado que recuerda las fachadas de los palacetes históricos de Lecce. La distribución de la casa con planta en L, se abre al jardín mediante grandes ventanales que permiten que la luz inunde los espacios. El porche, con sus arcos suaves, es el corazón de la vivienda. El color juega un papel clave. En el interior, se usaron tonos fuertes como rojo, verde y amarillo, presentes principalmente en telas y cortinas, pero también en mobiliario y detalles decorativos. Fuera, las ventanas verdes y el zócalo griego refuerzan la personalidad de la casa. Las fachadas blancas se enriquecen con el verde de los marcos y zócalos, mientras que los detalles en terracota, como los bajantes y las farolas, aportan calidez y autenticidad.

Bold reds, greens, and yellows define the interior, while green frames and terracotta details bring warmth and authenticity to the white facades.

MOCA ARQUITETURA

TWO LOST KIDS APARTMENT >

CURITIBA, BRAZIL

Photos: © Eduardo Macarios

TWO LOST KIDS APARTMENT

A universe of vibrant tones and flowing curves defines this 40 m^2 space designed for sisters Thalita and Gabriela Zukeram, the artistic duo behind "Two Lost Kids". Their visual identity, marked by a playful and nostalgic aesthetic, translates into an environment that serves both as a home and as a set for their video productions. The curving walls and furniture create a sense of continuous movement, enhancing the space's fluidity. "We wanted this place to feel like a portal into their universe, as if we had encapsulated their videos into a single room," explain the designers at Moca Arquitetura, the studio behind the project.
Color takes center stage. Among the most iconic elements are two Togo armchairs, a classic Michel Ducaroy design, placed in front of the curved wall separating the kitchen from the living area. Next to them, the "Ello" lamp—created by Moca—adds a play of transparency and reflections using wood, glass, and LED lighting. Appliances have been camouflaged to maintain visual harmony, while the television, with a matte finish and undulating frame, blends in as an artistic feature. The result: a vibrant retreat brimming with creativity and style.

Ein Universum aus kräftigen Farben und sanften Kurven prägt dieses 40 m^2 große Apartment, das für die Schwestern Thalita und Gabriela Zukeram – das Künstlerduo hinter „Two Lost Kids" – entworfen wurde. Ihre visuelle Identität, geprägt von einer verspielten und nostalgischen Ästhetik, spiegelt sich in einem Raum wider, der sowohl als Zuhause als auch als Filmset für ihre Videos dient. Die geschwungenen Wände und Möbel erzeugen ein Gefühl ständiger Bewegung und verstärken den fließenden Charakter des Raumes. „Wir wollten, dass dieser Ort wie ein Portal zu ihrer Welt wirkt – als hätten wir ihre Videos in einem einzigen Raum eingefangen", erklären die Architektinnen von Moca Arquitetura.
Farbe spielt die Hauptrolle: Zwei ikonische „Togo"-Sessel von Michel Ducaroy stehen vor einer geschwungenen Wand, die Küche und Wohnzimmer trennt. Daneben fügt die von Moca entworfene „Ello"-Lampe mit Holz, Glas und LEDs ein spannendes Spiel aus Transparenzen und Reflexionen hinzu. Die Elektrogeräte sind dezent integriert, um die visuelle Harmonie nicht zu stören, während der matte, wellenförmig gerahmte Fernseher sich als künstlerisches Element ins Gesamtbild einfügt. Das Ergebnis: ein lebendiges Refugium voller Kreativität und Stil.

Un univers de tons vibrants et de courbes enveloppantes définit cet espace de 40 m^2 conçu pour les sœurs Thalita et Gabriela Zukeram, le duo d'artistes à l'origine de « Two Lost Kids ». Leur identité visuelle, marquée par une esthétique ludique et nostalgique, se traduit par un environnement qui fonctionne à la fois comme une maison et comme un plateau d'enregistrement pour leurs vidéos. Les sinuosités des murs et du mobilier créent une impression de mouvement continu, renforçant la fluidité de l'espace. « Nous voulions que cet endroit soit comme un portail vers son univers, comme si nous avions encapsulé ses vidéos dans une seule pièce », explique Moca Arquitetura, le studio en charge du projet.
La couleur est le protagoniste incontesté. Parmi les éléments les plus emblématiques, on trouve deux fauteuils « Togo », un classique de Michel Ducaroy, placés devant le mur courbe qui sépare la cuisine du salon. À côté d'eux, la lampe « Ello », créée par Moca, ajoute un jeu de transparences et de reflets avec le bois, le verre et les LED. Les appareils électriques ont été camouflés pour ne pas rompre l'harmonie visuelle, tandis que la télévision, avec sa finition mate et son cadre ondulé, est intégrée comme une œuvre d'art. Le résultat : une retraite vivante qui respire la créativité et le style.

Un universo de tonos vibrantes y curvas envolventes define este espacio de 40 m^2 diseñado para las hermanas Thalita y Gabriela Zukeram, el dúo de artistas detrás de «Two Lost Kids». Su identidad visual, marcada por una estética lúdica y nostálgica, se traduce en un ambiente que funciona como hogar y como set de grabación para sus videos. La sinuosidad en los muros y el mobiliario crea una sensación de movimiento continuo, reforzando la fluidez del espacio. «Queríamos que este lugar se sintiera como un portal a su universo, como si hubiéramos encapsulado sus videos en una sola habitación», explican desde Moca Arquitetura, el estudio a cargo del proyecto.
El color es el protagonista indiscutible. Entre los elementos más icónicos destacan dos butacas «Togo», diseño clásico de Michel Ducaroy, ubicadas frente al muro curvo que separa la cocina del salón. Junto a ellas, la lámpara «Ello», creada por Moca, suma un juego de transparencias y reflejos con madera, vidrio y LED. Los electrodomésticos se han camuflado para no romper la armonía visual, mientras que la televisión, con acabado mate y enmarcado ondulado, se integra como una pieza artística. El resultado: un refugio vibrante que destila creatividad y estilo.

Color takes center stage in this artist space, defined by a playful and nostalgic aesthetic.

FAMILY HOUSE IN MAARSSEN >

UTRECHT, THE NETHERLANDS

Photos: © Anouk Moerman Photography

FAMILY HOUSE IN MAARSSEN

The owners of this home opted for a bold and vibrant vision for their house. With the idea that each space should reflect its own personality, they embraced Nox Studio Interiors's proposal to infuse each corner with a palette of intense tones. The real challenge lay in maintaining harmony, ensuring that the explosion of color didn't feel overwhelming or chaotic. The key, therefore, was to integrate the tones in such a way that each room felt unique without losing the sense of being part of a whole.
However, color is not the only protagonist. Graphic elements, present in surfaces such as the hallway and bathroom, as well as textiles, add an extra layer of dynamism. A notable example is the tiger figure in the entrance hall carpet, which surprises and leaves a lasting impression of personality. The careful selection of prints and patterns ensures that the colors are reflected subtly and fluidly in each room. This way, each tone complements the next, creating natural transitions that form a cohesive and dynamic environment. The result is a home full of life and energy, inviting one to enjoy each day.

Die Eigentümer dieses Hauses setzten auf eine mutige und lebendige Vision für ihr Zuhause. Mit der Idee, dass jeder Raum seine eigene Persönlichkeit widerspiegelt, nahmen sie den Vorschlag von Nox Studio Interiors an, jedem Bereich eine intensive Farbpalette zu verleihen. Die eigentliche Herausforderung bestand darin, die Harmonie zu bewahren und sicherzustellen, dass die Farbexplosion weder überwältigend noch chaotisch wirkt. Der Schlüssel lag darin, die Farbtöne so zu integrieren, dass sich jeder Raum einzigartig anfühlt, ohne das Gefühl zu verlieren, Teil eines Ganzen zu sein.
Doch nicht nur Farbe spielt eine Hauptrolle. Grafische Elemente, die auf Oberflächen wie dem Eingangsbereich und dem Badezimmer zu finden sind, sowie Textilien verleihen dem Design eine zusätzliche dynamische Ebene. Ein herausragendes Beispiel ist die Tigerfigur auf dem Teppich in der Eingangshalle, die überrascht und Persönlichkeit verleiht. Die sorgfältige Auswahl von Mustern und Designs sorgt dafür, dass sich die Farben in jedem Raum subtil und fließend widerspiegeln. So ergänzt jeder Farbton den nächsten und schafft natürliche Übergänge, die eine kohärente und dynamische Atmosphäre erzeugen. Das Ergebnis ist ein Zuhause voller Leben und Energie, das dazu einlädt, jeden Tag zu genießen.

Les propriétaires de cette maison ont opté pour une vision audacieuse et vibrante de leur foyer. Souhaitant que chaque espace reflète sa propre personnalité, ils ont accepté la proposition de Nox Studio Interiors d'infuser chaque recoin d'une palette de tons intenses. Le véritable défi résidait dans le maintien de l'harmonie, en s'assurant que cette explosion de couleurs ne devienne ni accablante ni chaotique. Ainsi, l'essentiel était d'intégrer les teintes de manière à ce que chaque pièce ait son caractère unique tout en conservant une sensation d'unité.
Cependant, la couleur n'est pas la seule protagoniste. Les éléments graphiques, présents sur des surfaces comme le hall d'entrée et la salle de bains, ainsi que les textiles, ajoutent une couche supplémentaire de dynamisme. Un exemple marquant est la figure du tigre sur le tapis du hall d'entrée, une touche surprenante qui imprime une forte personnalité. Le choix soigneux des motifs et des imprimés garantit une transition fluide des couleurs dans chaque pièce. Ainsi, chaque teinte complète la suivante, créant des transitions naturelles qui confèrent à l'ensemble une atmosphère cohérente et dynamique. Le résultat est une maison pleine de vie et d'énergie, qui invite à profiter de chaque instant.

Los propietarios de esta vivienda apostaron por una visión audaz y vibrante para su hogar. Con la idea de que cada espacio reflejara su propia personalidad, aceptaron la propuesta de Nox Studio Interiors de infundir a cada rincón una paleta de tonos intensos. El verdadero reto radicaba en mantener la armonía, asegurando que la explosión de color no resultara abrumadora ni caótica. Así, la clave fue integrar los tonos de manera que cada habitación se sintiera única sin perder la sensación de formar parte de un todo.
El color, sin embargo, no es el único protagonista. Los elementos gráficos, presentes en superficies como el recibidor y el baño, y los textiles, aportan una capa extra de dinamismo. Un ejemplo que destaca es la figura del tigre en la alfombra del hall de acceso, que sorprende e imprime una personalidad. La selección cuidadosa de estampados y patrones garantiza que los colores se reflejen de manera sutil y fluida en cada habitación. De esta manera, cada tono complementa al siguiente, logrando transiciones naturales que crean un ambiente cohesivo y dinámico. El resultado es un hogar lleno de vida y energía, que invita a disfrutar de cada día.

JAIPUR SPLENDOR
HET BOEK

Color isn't the only focus. Graphic elements, found on surfaces and paired with textiles, add an extra layer of dynamism

PRACOWNIA DUŻY POKÓJ

CHEERFUL COLORS IN BYDGOSZCZ >

BYDGOSZCZ, POLAND

Photos: © Natalia Kaczmarek - Inkadr.pl

Brighton
England

CHEERFUL COLORS IN BYDGOSZCZ

The vibrant energy of the homeowners set the tone for this apartment renovation, achieved through a combination of colors and design pieces. After living in Brighton (UK), the couple returned to Poland with a clear vision: to preserve the character of their home while integrating their artistic sensitivity and love for vintage style. Located in a 1970s building, the apartment maintains its essence thanks to a respectful restoration. The original parquet was revitalized, woodwork restored, and baseboards faithfully replicated by a craftsman. The walls, barely altered, retain their history, while armchairs, chairs, and sofas received new upholstery. Color plays the leading role. The kitchen shines in a sunny yellow, setting the tone for the rest of the palette. In the hallway, the coral-colored ceiling surprises with its bold warmth, while patterned wallpaper on the living room ceiling adds a touch of whimsy. The layout was also modified: the former kitchen became a child's bedroom, while the living room was transformed into a spacious kitchen-dining area. As a finishing touch, a Brighton poster in the living room pays homage to the city that influenced its design and holds precious memories.

Die lebendige Energie der Eigentümer bestimmte den Ton der Renovierung dieser Wohnung durch eine Kombination aus Farben und Designstücken. Nach Jahren in Brighton (Vereinigtes Königreich) kehrte das Paar nach Polen zurück – mit einer klaren Vision: den Charakter ihres Zuhauses zu bewahren und gleichzeitig ihre künstlerische Sensibilität sowie ihre Liebe zum Vintage-Stil zu integrieren. Die Wohnung, die sich in einem Gebäude aus den 1970er Jahren befindet, bewahrt ihren ursprünglichen Charme dank einer behutsamen Restaurierung. Der originale Parkettboden wurde revitalisiert, die Tischlerarbeiten restauriert und die Sockelleisten von einem Kunsthandwerker originalgetreu nachgebildet. Die Wände blieben nahezu unberührt, um ihre Geschichte zu bewahren, während Sessel, Stühle und Sofas neu gepolstert wurden. Farbe spielt die Hauptrolle: Die Küche erstrahlt in einem sonnigen Gelb, das den Farbton für das gesamte Konzept vorgab. Im Flur überrascht die korallenfarbene Decke mit ihrer warmen Intensität, während eine gemusterte Tapete an der Wohnzimmerdecke eine fantasievolle Note hinzufügt. Auch die Raumaufteilung wurde verändert: Die ehemalige Küche wurde in ein Kinderzimmer umgewandelt, und das Wohnzimmer dient nun als großzügige Wohnküche. Als letztes Detail zollt ein Brighton-Poster im Wohnzimmer der Stadt Tribut, die ihr Design und ihre wertvollen Erinnerungen geprägt hat.

L'énergie vibrante des propriétaires a donné le ton à la rénovation de cet appartement grâce à l'association de couleurs et de pièces de design. Après avoir vécu à Brighton (Royaume-Uni), le couple est rentré en Pologne avec une vision claire : préserver le caractère de leur maison, en intégrant leur sensibilité artistique et leur amour du vintage. Installé dans un immeuble des années 1970, l'appartement conserve son essence grâce à une restauration respectueuse. Le parquet d'origine a été ravivé, les boiseries récupérées et les plinthes fidèlement reproduites par un artisan. Les murs, à peine touchés, conservent leur histoire, tandis que les fauteuils, les chaises et les canapés ont été retapissés. La couleur est le principal protagoniste. La cuisine brille dans un jaune ensoleillé qui donne le ton au reste de la palette. Dans le couloir, le plafond couleur corail surprend par sa chaleur audacieuse, tandis qu'un papier peint sur le plafond du salon ajoute une touche de fantaisie. L'agencement a également changé : l'ancienne cuisine est devenue une chambre d'enfant, et le salon a été transformé en une spacieuse cuisine-salle à manger. En guise de touche finale, un poster de Brighton dans le salon rend hommage à la ville qui a influencé sa conception et ses souvenirs.

La energía vibrante de los propietarios marcaron el tono de la renovación de este apartamento a través de la combinación de colores y piezas de diseño. Tras vivir en Brighton (Reino Unido), la pareja regresó a Polonia con una visión clara: preservar el carácter de su hogar, integrando su sensibilidad artística y su amor por lo vintage. Ubicado en un edificio de los años 70, el apartamento mantiene su esencia gracias a una restauración respetuosa. El parquet original fue revitalizado, la carpintería recuperada y los rodapiés replicados fielmente por un artesano. Las paredes, apenas intervenidas, conservan su historia, mientras que butacas, sillas y sofás recibieron nuevos tapizados. El color es el gran protagonista. La cocina brilla en un amarillo soleado que marcó el rumbo del resto de la paleta. En el pasillo, el techo en color coral sorprende con su audaz calidez, mientras que un papel pintado en el techo del salón añade una capa de fantasía. La distribución también cambió: la antigua cocina ahora es un dormitorio infantil, y el salón se transformó en una amplia cocina-comedor. Como broche final, un póster de Brighton en el salón rinde homenaje a la ciudad que influyó en su diseño y en sus recuerdos preciados.

The combination of colors and design pieces reflects the vibrant energy of the owners in the apartment renovation.

ROOM SERVICE STUDIO

JEAN-JACQUES ROUSSEAU >

LILLE, FRANCE

Photos: © Chaleur Production for Julien Richardson

Muller Van Severen

JEAN-JACQUES ROUSSEAU

This co-living space for IvyNest, located in Lille, a charming city in northern France known for its gray weather, redefines the concept of shared spaces with a bold use of color. In the three-story main house, each floor is assigned a unique tone reflecting nature, bringing vitality to an environment with little sunlight.
On the first floor, the rooms are decorated in green, evoking the image of grass. The second floor is dominated by blue, representing the sky, while the third floor features shades of orange and yellow, symbolizing the sun. Each bedroom has a colored accent wall behind the bed, while the remaining walls are painted in Winborne White to balance the atmosphere. In the independent studio, a neutral shade, Terre Cuite brown, was chosen for its calming effect. For accents, bright yellow was used for the lighting fixtures and the Moustache chair. The bathrooms follow a similar approach, with red-edged tile details that not only serve their purpose but also act as a refined design statement, maintaining serenity and visual cohesion throughout the space.

Dieses Co-Living-Projekt für IvyNest in Lille, einer charmanten Stadt im Norden Frankreichs mit oft grauem Himmel, definiert das Konzept des gemeinschaftlichen Wohnens durch den kühnen Einsatz von Farbe neu. Im dreistöckigen Hauptgebäude hat jede Etage eine eigene Farbwelt, die von der Natur inspiriert ist und das lichtarme Klima mit Lebendigkeit ausgleicht.
Im ersten Stock sind die Zimmer in Grün gehalten und erinnern an saftige Wiesen. Die zweite Etage wird von Blau dominiert, das den Himmel symbolisiert, während die dritte Etage mit Orange- und Gelbtönen das Sonnenlicht einfängt. Hinter jedem Bett hebt sich eine farbige Wand ab, während die restlichen Wände in „Winborne White" gestrichen sind, um die Atmosphäre auszugleichen. Im separaten Studio entschied man sich für einen neutralen Ton – „Terre Cuite"-Braun –, der eine beruhigende Wirkung hat. Akzente setzen leuchtend gelbe Leuchten und der Stuhl „Moustache". Die Badezimmer folgen demselben gestalterischen Prinzip, wobei rote Kachelkonturen als elegantes Designelement dienen, das die visuelle Kohärenz im gesamten Raum bewahrt.

Cet co-living pour IvyNest, situé à Lille, une charmante ville du nord de la France connue pour son climat gris, redéfinit le concept d'espace partagé avec une application audacieuse de la couleur. Dans la maison principale, sur trois niveaux, chaque étage a un ton unique qui reflète la nature, cherchant à apporter de la vitalité à un environnement peu ensoleillé.
Au premier étage, les chambres sont décorées en vert, évoquant l'image de l'herbe. Le premier étage est dominé par le bleu, qui représente le ciel, et le troisième étage, par des nuances d'orange et de jaune, qui symbolisent le soleil. Les murs de chaque chambre ont une couleur de fond derrière le lit, et le reste est peint en blanc Winborne pour équilibrer l'atmosphère. Dans le bureau séparé, on a choisi un ton neutre, le brun Terre Cuite, qui a un effet calmant. Pour les détails, un jaune vif a été choisi pour les luminaires et la chaise Moustache. La conception des salles de bains suit une ligne similaire, soulignée par des détails dans les carreaux profilés rouges, qui non seulement remplissent leur fonction mais deviennent également un acte de design élégant, en maintenant toujours la sérénité et la cohésion visuelle dans tout l'espace.

Este co-living para IvyNest, situado en Lille, una encantadora ciudad del norte de Francia conocida por su clima gris, redefine el concepto de espacio compartido con una audaz aplicación del color. En la casa principal, de tres niveles, cada planta tiene un tono único que refleja la naturaleza, buscando aportar vitalidad a un entorno con escaso sol.
En el primer piso, las habitaciones están decoradas en verde, evocando la imagen del césped. El segundo piso está dominado por el azul, representando el cielo, y el tercer piso, con tonos de naranja y amarillo, que simbolizan el sol. Las paredes de cada habitación tienen un color de fondo detrás de la cama, y el resto están pintadas en blanco Winborne para equilibrar la atmósfera. En el estudio independiente, se optó por un tono neutro, el marrón Terre Cuite, que tiene un efecto calmante. Para los detalles, se eligió un amarillo brillante en las luminarias y la silla Moustache. El diseño de los baños sigue una línea similar, destacando con detalles en los azulejos perfilados en rojo, que no solo cumplen su función sino que se convierten en un acto de diseño elegante, manteniendo siempre la serenidad y la cohesión visual en todo el espacio.

La Cucina

Paul Klee

GILLIS RESIDENCE >

AMSTERDAM, THE NETHERLANDS

Photos: © Nina van Ewijk, Geertje van Odijk

Polyester

GILLIS RESIDENCE

This 85 m^2 apartment in Amsterdam West merges past, present, and future, blending the aesthetics of India Mahdavi with The Jetsons. The result is a playful interpretation of a mid-century home projected into the future.
The design takes full advantage of the natural light streaming in through the double doors at the front of the apartment, creating an open-plan space that houses the kitchen, dining area, and cocktail lounge. The bubblegum pink kitchen serves as the focal point, complemented by retro-futuristic details such as the ring accents on table legs and Louis Poulsen lamps. The cocktail area stands out with its green wallpaper, adding rich texture and a luxurious feel to the space. Curved furniture and a custom blue rug enhance the comfort and style. The low ceiling in this corner creates a cocooning effect, while vintage lamps and chrome details—such as mirrors and Sputnik lamps—bring in a retro-futuristic vibe. Private areas, including the bedroom and bathroom, offer a tranquil retreat with soft hues that contrast with the vibrant common areas, fostering complete relaxation.

Diese 85 m^2 große Wohnung in Amsterdam-West vereint Vergangenheit, Gegenwart und Zukunft – eine Mischung aus India Mahdavis Ästhetik und den Jetsons. Das Ergebnis ist eine verspielte Interpretation eines Mid-Century-Heims mit futuristischem Flair.
Das Design nutzt das natürliche Licht, das durch die Flügeltüren an der Vorderseite der Wohnung strömt, und schafft einen offenen Grundriss mit Küche, Essbereich und Cocktail-Lounge. Die Kaugummi-rosa Küche ist das Herzstück des Raumes und wird durch retro-futuristische Details wie die ringförmigen Tischbeine und „Louis Poulsen"-Leuchten ergänzt. Der Cocktailbereich wird durch eine grüne Tapete geprägt, die dem Raum eine luxuriöse Textur verleiht. Geschwungene Möbel und ein maßgefertigter blauer Teppich sorgen für Komfort und Stil. Die niedrige Decke in diesem Bereich erzeugt ein einhüllendes Gefühl, während Vintage-Lampen und chromfarbene Details – wie Spiegel und Sputnik-Leuchten – einen futuristischen Retro-Touch hinzufügen. Die privaten Bereiche, wie das Schlafzimmer und das Badezimmer, bieten dagegen einen ruhigen Rückzugsort mit sanften Farben, die einen Kontrast zu den lebhaften Gemeinschaftsräumen bilden und eine vollständige Entspannung ermöglichen.

Cet appartement de 85 m^2 situé dans l'ouest d'Amsterdam fusionne le passé, le présent et le futur, en combinant l'esthétique d'India Mahdavi avec celle des Jetsons. Le résultat est une interprétation amusante d'une maison du milieu du siècle qui s'inscrit dans le futur.
Le design tire parti de la lumière naturelle qui traverse les doubles portes à l'avant de l'appartement, créant un espace ouvert qui abrite la cuisine, la salle à manger et l'espace cocktail. La cuisine, en rose bubblegum, occupe le devant de la scène et est complétée par des détails rétro-futuristes tels que les anneaux sur les pieds de table et les lampes Louis Poulsen. Le coin cocktail, avec son papier peint vert, ajoute une texture riche et luxueuse à l'espace. Le mobilier incurvé et la moquette bleue personnalisée ajoutent une couche de confort et de style. Le plafond bas de ce coin crée une atmosphère enveloppante, tandis que les lampes vintage et les accents chromés, tels que les miroirs et les lampes Sputnik, ajoutent une touche rétro futuriste. Les espaces privés, tels que la chambre et la salle de bains, offrent une retraite tranquille et enveloppante, avec des couleurs douces qui contrastent avec les espaces communs, encourageant une déconnexion totale.

Este apartamento de 85 m^2 en Amsterdam West fusiona el pasado, el presente y el futuro, combinando la estética de India Mahdavi con los Jetsons. El resultado es una divertida interpretación de un hogar *mid-century* llevado al futuro.
El diseño aprovecha la luz natural que entra por las puertas dobles al frente del apartamento, creando un espacio de planta abierta que alberga la cocina, el comedor y la zona de cócteles. La cocina, en rosa chicle, es el centro de atención y se complementa con detalles retro-futuristas como los anillos en las patas de las mesas y las lámparas Louis Poulsen. El área de cócteles, destaca por su papel-tapiz verde, que aporta una textura rica y lujosa al espacio. Los muebles curvos y la alfombra azul personalizada añaden una capa de confort y estilo. El techo bajo en este rincón crea una sensación envolvente, mientras que las lámparas vintage y los detalles cromados, como los espejos y las lámparas Sputnik, aportan un aire retro futurista. Las áreas privadas, como el dormitorio y el baño, ofrecen un refugio tranquilo y envolvente, con colores suaves que contrastan con las zonas comunes, fomentando la desconexión total.

SMEG

Polyester

The result of this apartment's renovation is a playful interpretation of a mid-century home brought into the future.

STUDIO BOSKO

CHROMA PENTHOUSE >

BERLIN, GERMANY

Photos: © Giulia Maretti Studio

11 20

CHROMA PENTHOUSE

The interior design of this penthouse in Kreuzberg, Berlin, responds to the needs of a young couple recently arrived from Amsterdam. The owners bought the house during the initial construction phase, just before the COVID pandemic, with the idea of creating a multifunctional home with "as little white as possible". She, an illustrator, and he, with a colour blindness that only allowed him to see intense colours, were instrumental in choosing a palette based on primary colours. Thus the kitchen took on an intense yellow, the dining room was dyed red and the living room was wrapped in a deep green. The private areas, on the other hand, were defined with a softer, more nuanced atmosphere. One of the key pieces was Coco Davez's Frank Zappa painting, which the clients brought with them. Because of the painting's expressive power it was clear that it would occupy a prominent place, and the designer, Kasia Kronberger, decided to put it in dialogue with the kitchen to add tension to the space. The furnishings are part of a varied ensemble with pieces in different styles that are eye-catching. In the dining room and living room, the vintage Vico Magistretti Carimate chairs and the Camaleonda sofa in pine green mohair alpaca complete a functional, cosy atmosphere full of personality.

Die Inneneinrichtung dieses Penthouses in Berlin-Kreuzberg entspricht den Bedürfnissen eines jungen Paares, das vor kurzem aus Amsterdam gekommen ist. Die Eigentümer kauften das Haus in der ersten Bauphase, kurz vor der COVID-Pandemie, mit der Idee, ein multifunktionales Haus mit „so wenig Weiß wie möglich" zu schaffen. Sie, eine Illustratorin, und er, der aufgrund seiner Farbenblindheit nur intensive Farben sehen kann, waren maßgeblich an der Auswahl einer auf Primärfarben basierenden Farbpalette beteiligt. So erhielt die Küche ein intensives Gelb, das Esszimmer wurde rot eingefärbt und das Wohnzimmer in ein tiefes Grün gehüllt. Die privaten Bereiche hingegen wurden mit einer weicheren, nuancierteren Atmosphäre gestaltet. Eines der Schlüsselstücke war das Frank-Zappa-Gemälde von Coco Davez, das die Kunden mitbrachten. Aufgrund der Ausdruckskraft des Gemäldes war es klar, dass es einen prominenten Platz einnehmen würde, und die Designerin Kasia Kronberger beschloss, es in einen Dialog mit der Küche zu setzen, um dem Raum Spannung zu verleihen. Das Mobiliar ist Teil eines abwechslungsreichen Ensembles mit Stücken in verschiedenen Stilen, die einen Blickfang darstellen. Im Esszimmer und im Wohnzimmer vervollständigen die Vintage-Stühle Vico Magistretti Carimate und das Sofa Camaleonda aus tannengrünem Mohair-Alpaka eine funktionelle und gemütliche Atmosphäre voller Persönlichkeit.

La décoration intérieure de ce penthouse à Kreuzberg, Berlin, répond aux besoins d'un jeune couple récemment arrivé d'Amsterdam. Les propriétaires ont acheté la maison pendant la phase initiale de construction, juste avant la pandémie de COVID, avec l'idée de créer une maison multifonctionnelle avec « le moins de blanc possible ». Elle, illustratrice, et lui, daltonien qui ne voit que les couleurs intenses, ont joué un rôle déterminant dans le choix d'une palette basée sur les couleurs primaires. Ainsi, la cuisine a pris un jaune intense, la salle à manger s'est teintée de rouge et le salon s'est enveloppé d'un vert profond. Les espaces privés, en revanche, ont été définis par une atmosphère plus douce et plus nuancée. L'une des pièces maîtresses était le tableau de Frank Zappa de Coco Davez, que les clients avaient apporté avec eux. En raison de la puissance expressive du tableau, il était évident qu'il occuperait une place de choix, et la designer, Kasia Kronberger, a décidé de le faire dialoguer avec la cuisine pour ajouter de la tension à l'espace. Le mobilier fait partie d'un ensemble varié avec des pièces de styles différents qui attirent l'attention. Dans la salle à manger et le salon, les chaises vintage Vico Magistretti Carimate et le canapé Camaleonda en mohair alpaga vert pin complètent une atmosphère fonctionnelle, accueillante et pleine de personnalité.

El diseño interior de este ático en Kreuzberg, Berlín, responde a las necesidades de una pareja joven recién llegada desde Ámsterdam. Los propietarios adquirieron la vivienda durante la fase inicial de construcción, justo antes de la pandemia de COVID, con la idea de crear un hogar multifuncional con «lo menos blanco posible». Ella, ilustradora, y él, con un daltonismo que solo le permitía ver colores intensos, fueron decisivos para la elección de una paleta basada en colores primarios. Es así como la cocina adoptó un amarillo intenso, el comedor se tiñó de rojo y la sala de estar se envolvió en un verde profundo. Las áreas privadas, en cambio, se definieron con una atmósfera más suave y matizada. Una de las piezas clave fue la obra de Frank Zappa, de Coco Davez, que los clientes trajeron consigo. Gracias a la fuerza expresiva del cuadro estaba claro que ocuparía un sitio prominente, y la diseñadora Kasia Kronberger, decidió ponerlo en diálogo con la cocina para añadir tensión al espacio. El mobiliario forma parte de un conjunto variado con piezas de diferentes estilos que resultan llamativas. En el comedor y la sala de estar, destacan las sillas vintage Vico Magistretti Carimate y el sofá Camaleonda en alpaca mohair verde pino, terminan de definir un ambiente funcional, acogedor y lleno de personalidad.

The search for a multifunctional and vibrant home for a young couple led to a palette of primary colors, deliberately avoiding white.

DON'T DWELL ON YOUR FUCK-UPS
EFFICIENTLY, USE REFERENCES WHEN STUCK
BILDERBERG KONFERENZ
24/25 SEPTEMBER
UGH
LOVE & ROCKETS

STUDIO HOLLOND

RAINBOW COUNTRY HOME IN SUSSEX >

SUSSEX, UNITED KINGDOM

Photos: © Tom Mannion

RAINBOW COUNTRY HOME IN SUSSEX

The renovation of this home reflects the identity of a couple and their children: she, with a bohemian and artistic style, and he, with a preference for simplicity and order. The most significant intervention was the creation of two central areas: an open-plan living room-library and a kitchen-dining area. The use of color is one of the most striking features. A green-framed mirror placed above the fireplace serves as the focal point of the living room. The fireplace pattern, inspired by Missoni's designs, introduces a graphic and visually engaging element.
In the kitchen, the white marble floor with salmon-pink details softens the ambiance, while the red-and-white striped Claremont curtains provide a playful contrast without overwhelming the space. The walls, painted in soft tones—chartreuse in the library and blue in the master bedroom—act as a subtle backdrop, allowing the colors and details to shine. Notable details include the Fortuny silk lamp hanging over the hallway and a mural inspired by Saul Steinberg in the children's bathroom. Custom pieces, such as the spiral chairs and the green mirror, reinforce the dominant eclectic aesthetic.

Die Renovierung dieses Hauses spiegelt die Identität eines Paares und ihrer Kinder wider: Sie mit einem bohemien und künstlerischen Stil, er mit einer Vorliebe für Einfachheit und Ordnung. Die bedeutendste Veränderung war die Schaffung von zwei zentralen Bereichen: eines offenen Wohnzimmers mit Bibliothek und einer Wohnküche. Die Verwendung von Farbe ist eines der herausragendsten Merkmale. Der Spiegel mit grünen Rahmen über dem Kamin zieht im Wohnzimmer alle Blicke auf sich. Das Muster auf dem Kamin, inspiriert von den Designs von Missoni, bringt eine grafische und visuell ansprechende Note.
In der Küche sorgt der weiße Marmorboden mit lachsrosa Details für eine sanfte Atmosphäre, während die rot-weiß gestreiften Vorhänge von Claremont einen verspielten Kontrast setzen, ohne zu überladen. Die Wände sind in sanften Tönen gestrichen, wie Chartreuse in der Bibliothek und Blau im Hauptschlafzimmer, und dienen als dezenter Hintergrund, der Farben und Details zum Leuchten bringt. Besondere Akzente setzen die Fortuny-Seidenlampe, die im Flur hängt, und ein Wandgemälde, inspiriert von Saul Steinberg, im Kinderbad. Maßgefertigte Stücke wie die spiralförmigen Stühle und der grüne Spiegel verstärken die dominante eklektische Ästhetik.

La rénovation de cette maison reflète l'identité d'un couple et de leurs enfants : elle, avec un style bohème et artistique, et lui, avec une préférence pour la simplicité et l'ordre. L'intervention la plus importante a été la création de deux espaces centraux : un salon/bibliothèque ouvert et une cuisine/salle à manger. L'utilisation de la couleur est l'un des points forts. Le miroir encadré de vert au-dessus de la cheminée est le point focal du salon. Le motif de la cheminée, inspiré des motifs Missoni, apporte une touche graphique et visuellement attrayante.
Dans la cuisine, le sol en marbre blanc aux accents rose saumoné adoucit l'ambiance, tandis que les rideaux rayés rouges et blancs de Claremont apportent un contraste ludique sans surcharge. Les murs peints dans des tons doux, comme la chartreuse dans la bibliothèque et le bleu dans la chambre principale, servent de toile de fond subtile qui laisse transparaître les couleurs et les détails. Le lustre en soie Fortuny suspendu dans le couloir et la peinture murale inspirée de Saul Steinberg dans la salle de bains des enfants en sont des exemples. Les pièces personnalisées, telles que les chaises en spirale et le miroir vert, renforcent l'esthétique éclectique dominante.

La reforma de esta casa refleja la identidad de una pareja y sus hijos: ella, con un estilo bohemio y artístico y él, con una preferencia por la simplicidad y el orden. La intervención más significativa fue la creación de dos áreas centrales: un salón-biblioteca de planta abierta y una cocina-comedor. El uso del color es uno de los puntos más destacados. El espejo con marcos verdes colocado sobre la chimenea, es el centro de atención del salón. El estampado en la chimenea, inspirado en los patrones de Missoni, introduce un toque gráfico y visualmente atractivo.
En la cocina, el suelo de mármol blanco con detalles en rosa salmón suaviza el ambiente, mientras que las cortinas a rayas rojas y blancas, de Claremont, aportan un contraste lúdico sin recargar. Las paredes pintadas en tonos suaves, como el chartreuse en la biblioteca y el azul en el dormitorio principal, sirven como un fondo sutil que deja que los colores y los detalles resplandezcan. Destacan detalles como la lámpara de seda Fortuny que cuelga sobre el pasillo y un mural inspirado en Saul Steinberg en el baño infantil. Las piezas personalizadas, como las sillas espirales y el espejo verde, refuerzan la estética ecléctica dominante.

AGA

In the renovation of this house, the use of color is one of the standout features, with an eclectic aesthetic as the dominant style.

Modern Painting and Sculpture
in the Home of Mr Jim Ede
KETTLE'S YARD
UNIVERSITY OF CAMBRIDGE
BARNEY
CIRCUS

STUDIO MILO

BOSCO VERTICALE >

MILAN, ITALY

Photos: © Monica Spezia

BOSCO VERTICALE

On the 23rd floor of Bosco Verticale, one of Milan's most unique skyscrapers, the vegetation envelops the skyline, offering the sensation of living among the clouds. Designed by Stefano Boeri, this iconic building redefines the relationship between architecture and nature. Despite its lush surroundings, the 300 m² flat initially presented an aesthetic lacking in character. So, the owners—a cosmopolitan couple who divide their lives between Miami and Europe—turned to Studio MILO, known for infusing each space with an Italian design identity, complemented by international influences. The brief was clear: a unique, colorful interior with a distinctive design imprint. The entrance reveals bespoke cupboards lined with plant-motif wallpaper, establishing a subtle dialogue with the exterior. A sliding door, specifically designed for the project, separates the kitchen from the social area, preserving visual continuity. The selection of furniture and textiles, the result of careful research, encompasses both iconic and contemporary pieces. From lamps to rugs to small decorative objects, each element contributes to a balanced composition that blends styles, giving character and coherence to the space as a whole.

Im 23. Stock des Bosco Verticale, einem der einzigartigsten Wolkenkratzer Mailands, umhüllt die Vegetation die Skyline, und man hat das Gefühl, zwischen den Wolken zu leben. Dieses von Stefano Boeri entworfene ikonische Gebäude definiert die Beziehung zwischen Architektur und Natur neu. Trotz der üppigen Umgebung wirkte die 300 Quadratmeter große Wohnung ästhetisch und charakterlos. Daher wandten sich die Eigentümer - ein kosmopolitisches Paar, das sein Leben zwischen Miami und Europa aufteilt - an das Studio MILO, das dafür bekannt ist, jedem Raum eine italienische Designidentität mit internationalen Einflüssen zu verleihen. Die Aufgabenstellung war klar: ein einzigartiges, farbenfrohes Interieur mit einer unverwechselbaren Designprägung. Im Eingangsbereich des Hauses befinden sich maßgefertigte Schränke, die mit Pflanzenmotivtapeten verkleidet sind und einen subtilen Dialog mit dem Außenbereich herstellen. Eine eigens für das Projekt entworfene Schiebetür trennt die Küche vom Sozialbereich und bewahrt die visuelle Kontinuität. Die Auswahl der Möbel und Textilien, die das Ergebnis einer sorgfältigen Recherche ist, umfasst sowohl ikonische als auch zeitgenössische Stücke. Von Lampen über Teppiche bis hin zu kleinen Dekorationsobjekten trägt jedes Element zu einer ausgewogenen Komposition bei, die Stile miteinander verbindet und dem Ganzen Charakter und Kohärenz verleiht.

Au 23e étage du Bosco Verticale, l'un des gratte-ciel les plus singuliers de Milan, la végétation enveloppe la ligne d'horizon et l'on a l'impression de vivre parmi les nuages. Conçu par Stefano Boeri, ce bâtiment emblématique redéfinit la relation entre l'architecture et la nature. Malgré son environnement luxuriant, l'appartement de 300 mètres carrés présentait une esthétique manquant de caractère. Les propriétaires — un couple cosmopolite qui partage sa vie entre Miami et l'Europe — se sont donc tournés vers le Studio MILO, connu pour donner à chaque espace une identité de design italien avec des influences internationales. Le cahier des charges était clair : un intérieur unique, coloré et marqué par un design distinctif. L'entrée de la maison révèle des placards sur mesure tapissés de papier peint à motif végétal, établissant un dialogue subtil avec l'extérieur. Une porte coulissante conçue spécialement pour le projet sépare la cuisine de l'espace social, préservant ainsi la continuité visuelle. La sélection de meubles et de textiles, fruit d'une recherche minutieuse, comprend des pièces iconiques et contemporaines. Des lampes aux tapis en passant par les petits objets décoratifs, chaque élément contribue à une composition équilibrée qui fusionne les styles, donnant caractère et cohérence à l'ensemble.

En el piso 23 de Bosco Verticale, uno de los rascacielos más singulares de Milán, la vegetación envuelve el horizonte, y se tiene la sensación de habitar entre las nubes. Diseñado por Stefano Boeri, este edificio icónico redefine la relación entre arquitectura y naturaleza. A pesar de su entorno exuberante, el apartamento de 300 metros cuadrados presentaba una estética carente de carácter. Por eso, los propietarios —una pareja cosmopolita que divide su vida entre Miami y Europa— confiaron en Studio MILO, conocido por imprimir a cada espacio una identidad de diseño italiano con influencias internacionales. La petición fue clara: un interior único, colorido y con una impronta de diseño distintiva. El acceso a la vivienda revela armarios a medida revestidos con papel pintado de motivos vegetales, estableciendo un sutil diálogo con el exterior. Una puerta corredera diseñada específicamente para el proyecto separa la cocina del área social, preservando la continuidad visual. La selección de mobiliario y textiles, resultado de una cuidadosa búsqueda, abarca piezas icónicas y contemporáneas. Desde lámparas hasta alfombras y pequeños objetos decorativos, cada elemento contribuye a una composición equilibrada que fusiona estilos, imprimiendo carácter y coherencia al conjunto.

Every element in this apartment was selected to balance styles, texture and colour, resulting in a space with both character and cohesion.

WOWOWA ARCHITECTURE

MAGIC >

MELBOURNE, AUSTRALIA
Photos: © Martina Gemmola

S,M,L,XL

MAGIC

The home of Monique and Scott Woodward, principals of WOWOWA Architecture, is a reflection of their playful and colourful approach to design. Purchased in 2016 in Northcote, the dwelling was a dilapidated former Californian bungalow that they transformed into a vibrant and welcoming home.
The project was carried out in two stages. First, urgent renovations were made to improve livability: foundation restructuring, insulation, hydronic heating and the conversion of a former sunroom into an en-suite bathroom. Years later, an extension was carried out. The most prominent element of the renovation is a six-metre glazed brick wall on the northern boundary, taking advantage of the orientation and previous renovations by neighbours. The colour palette, with magentas, browns and golds, evokes personal memories and creates an enveloping ambience. The rear façade design incorporates a decorative arch inspired by Moorish architecture and Californian bungalow style. This gesture reinforces the visual identity of the home, which the architects have christened Magic, a name that synthesises the transformation achieved and the desire to celebrate the extraordinary in everyday life.

Das Haus von Monique und Scott Woodward, den Inhabern von WOWOWA Architecture, spiegelt ihren verspielten und farbenfrohen Designansatz wider. Das 2016 in Northcote erworbene Haus war ein baufälliger ehemaliger kalifornischer Bungalow, den sie in ein lebendiges und einladendes Zuhause verwandelten.
Das Projekt wurde in zwei Phasen durchgeführt. Zunächst wurden dringende Renovierungsarbeiten durchgeführt, um die Wohnqualität zu verbessern: Sanierung des Fundaments, Isolierung, Warmwasserheizung und Umwandlung eines ehemaligen Sonnenzimmers in ein eigenes Badezimmer. Jahre später wurde eine Erweiterung durchgeführt. Das auffälligste Element der Renovierung ist eine sechs Meter lange verglaste Ziegelwand an der Nordgrenze, die die Ausrichtung und die früheren Renovierungen der Nachbarn nutzt. Die Farbpalette mit Magentatönen, Braun- und Goldtönen weckt persönliche Erinnerungen und schafft eine einladende Atmosphäre. Die Gestaltung der hinteren Fassade enthält einen dekorativen Bogen, der von der maurischen Architektur und dem kalifornischen Bungalowstil inspiriert ist. Diese Geste unterstreicht die visuelle Identität des Hauses, das die Architekten Magic getauft haben, ein Name, der die erreichte Transformation und den Wunsch, das Außergewöhnliche im täglichen Leben zu feiern, zusammenfasst.

La maison de Monique et Scott Woodward, directeurs de WOWOWA Architecture, reflète leur approche ludique et colorée du design. Achetée en 2016 à Northcote, l'habitation était un ancien bungalow californien délabré qu'ils ont transformé en une maison vibrante et accueillante.
Le projet a été réalisé en deux étapes. Tout d'abord, des rénovations urgentes ont été effectuées pour améliorer l'habitabilité : restructuration des fondations, isolation, chauffage hydronique et transformation d'un ancien solarium en salle de bain attenante. Des années plus tard, une extension a été réalisée. L'élément le plus marquant de la rénovation est un mur de briques vitrées de six mètres sur la limite nord, qui tire parti de l'orientation et des rénovations antérieures effectuées par les voisins. La couleur pal-ton-au-vue, avec des magentas, des bruns et des dorés, évoque des souvenirs personnels et crée une atmosphère d'enveloppement. La conception de la façade arrière intègre une arche décorative inspirée de l'architecture mauresque et du style bungalow californien. Ce geste renforce l'identité visuelle de la maison, que les architectes ont baptisée Magic, un nom qui synthétise la transformation réalisée et le désir de célébrer l'extraordinaire dans la vie de tous les jours.

La casa de Monique y Scott Woodward, directores de WOWOWA Architecture, es un reflejo de su enfoque lúdico y colorido en el diseño. Adquirida en 2016 en Northcote, la vivienda era un antiguo bungalow californiano en mal estado que transformaron en un hogar vibrante y acogedor.
El proyecto se llevó a cabo en dos etapas. Primero, se hizo las renovaciones urgentes para mejorar la habitabilidad: reestructuración de cimientos, aislamiento, calefacción hidrónica y la conversión de un antiguo solárium en un baño en suite. Años después se llevó a cabo una ampliación. El elemento más destacado de la reforma es un muro de ladrillo vidriado de seis metros en el límite norte, aprovechando la orientación y las renovaciones previas de los vecinos. La paleta de colores, con magentas, marrones y dorados, evoca recuerdos personales y crea un ambiente envolvente. El diseño de la fachada trasera incorpora un arco decorativo inspirado en la arquitectura morisca y en el estilo de los bungalows californianos. Este gesto refuerza la identidad visual del hogar, que los arquitectos han bautizado como Magic, un nombre que sintetiza la transformación lograda y el deseo de celebrar lo extraordinario en la vida cotidiana.

This home reflects the playful and colorful design approach of its owners, the designers behind WOWOWA Architecture

P. 60 < THE FIG TREE HOUSE

CONSTANZE LADNER

CONSTANZE LADNER

WIESBADEN, GERMANY
constanzeladner.de

Born and raised near Munich, Constanze Ladner worked for 18 years as a designer in the fashion industry, eventually becoming Head of Design at the streetwear brand Naketano. In 2018, she founded her own interior design studio. A self-taught designer, she is known for her passion for warm, natural materials—noble woods, stone, and ceramics—which she combines with diverse textures and a rich color palette to create harmonious aesthetics. Her approach is based on constant dialogue with her clients to craft sophisticated and cosmopolitan spaces, both residential and hospitality-focused, where elegance merges with a sense of security, harmony, and sensuality.

Née et élevée près de Munich, Constanze Ladner a travaillé pendant 18 ans en tant que designer dans l'industrie de la mode, occupant notamment le poste de responsable du design au sein de l'entreprise de streetwear Naketano. En 2018, elle a créé son propre studio de design d'intérieur. Autodidacte, elle se distingue par sa passion pour les matériaux chauds et naturels, les bois fins, la pierre et la céramique, qu'elle associe à diverses textures et à une riche palette chromatique pour obtenir une esthétique harmonieuse. Son approche est basée sur un dialogue constant avec ses clients pour créer des espaces résidentiels et d'accueil sophistiqués et cosmopolites, où l'élégance fusionne avec un sentiment de sécurité, d'harmonie et de sensualité.

Geboren und aufgewachsen in der Nähe von München, arbeitete Constanze Ladner 18 Jahre lang als Designerin in der Modeindustrie, zuletzt als Chefdesignerin bei der Streetwear-Marke Naketano. 2018 gründete sie ihr eigenes Interior-Design-Studio. Als Autodidaktin zeichnet sie sich durch ihre Leidenschaft für warme, natürliche Materialien aus – edle Hölzer, Stein und Keramik –, die sie mit vielfältigen Texturen und einer reichen Farbpalette kombiniert, um eine harmonische Ästhetik zu erschaffen. Ihr Ansatz basiert auf einem stetigen Dialog mit ihren Kunden, um raffinierte und kosmopolitische Räume zu gestalten – sowohl im Wohn- als auch im Gastgewerbebereich –, in denen Eleganz mit Geborgenheit, Harmonie und Sinnlichkeit verschmilzt.

Nacida y criada cerca de Múnich, Constanze Ladner trabajó durante 18 años como diseñadora en la industria de la moda, ocupando el puesto de jefa de diseño en la firma de streetwear Naketano. En 2018 creó su estudio de interiorismo. Autodidacta, se distingue por su pasión por materiales cálidos y naturales, maderas nobles, piedra y cerámica, que combina con texturas diversas y una paleta cromática rica para lograr una estética armoniosa. Su enfoque se basa en un diálogo constante con sus clientes para crear espacios sofisticados y cosmopolitas, residenciales y de hostelería, donde la elegancia se fusiona con la sensación de seguridad, armonía y sensualidad.

P. 68 < JACQUARD

CRAIE CRAIE

CÉLIA REUBRECHT

LYON, FRANCE
craiecraie.com

CRAIE CRAIE is an interior architecture studio founded by Célia Reubrecht, a graduate of the École d'Architecture d'Intérieur de Lyon. After gaining experience with various architects such as DPLG and interior designers, the designer decided to create her own studio, specialising in projects ranging from deep renovations to functional and harmonious decoration designs. The studio has a distinctive approach to the use of colour, applying it strategically to transform spaces and enhance the experience of those who inhabit them. La Maison CRAIE CRAIE is a shop that complements the studio's work with a selection of furniture and decorative objects.

CRAIE CRAIE est un studio d'architecture d'intérieur fondé par Célia Reubrecht, diplômée de l'École d'Architecture d'Intérieur de Lyon. Après avoir acquis de l'expérience auprès de différents architectes tels que DPLG et architectes d'intérieur, la designer a décidé de créer son propre studio, spécialisé dans des projets allant de la rénovation profonde à la décoration fonctionnelle et harmonieuse. Le studio a une approche distinctive de l'utilisation de la couleur, l'appliquant stratégiquement pour transformer les espaces et améliorer l'expérience de ceux qui les habitent. La Maison CRAIE CRAIE est une boutique qui complète le travail du studio avec une sélection de meubles et d'objets décoratifs.

CRAIE CRAIE ist ein Innenarchitekturbüro, das von Célia Reubrecht, einer Absolventin der École d'Architecture d'Intérieur de Lyon, gegründet wurde. Nachdem sie Erfahrungen bei verschiedenen Architekten wie DPLG und Innenarchitekten gesammelt hatte, beschloss die Designerin, ihr eigenes Studio zu gründen, das sich auf Projekte spezialisiert hat, die von tiefgreifenden Renovierungen bis zu funktionalen und harmonischen Dekorationsentwürfen reichen. Das Studio hat einen besonderen Ansatz für den Einsatz von Farben, indem es diese strategisch einsetzt, um Räume zu verändern und die Erfahrung derer, die sie bewohnen, zu verbessern. La Maison CRAIE CRAIE ist ein Geschäft, das die Arbeit des Studios mit einer Auswahl an Möbeln und Dekorationsobjekten ergänzt.

CRAIE CRAIE es un estudio de arquitectura de interiores fundado por Célia Reubrecht, graduada de la École d'Architecture d'Intérieur de Lyon. Tras adquirir experiencia con diversos arquitectos como DPLG y diseñadores de interiores, la diseñadora decidió crear su propio estudio, especializado en proyectos que van desde renovaciones profundas hasta diseños de decoración funcionales y armoniosos. El estudio tiene un enfoque distintivo en el uso del color, aplicándolo de manera estratégica para transformar espacios y mejorar la experiencia de quienes los habitan. La Maison CRAIE CRAIE es una tienda que complementa el trabajo del estudio con una selección de muebles y objetos de decoración.

P. 76 < SUPREMATISM AS INSPIRATION

DIHOME

YEVHENIIA SYTNIK

KYIV, UKRAINE
dihome.com.ua

Architect Yevheniia Sytnik founded her studio in 2016 with the aim of bringing to life design projects that fuse aesthetics and functionality. After training at the Academy of Construction and gaining experience at an architectural firm in Kyiv, she decided to create her own space to realise her vision. Since its inception, she has been able to consolidate a team of professionals who share her innovative approach and adapt to the needs of each client. The studio's philosophy seeks to design interiors that reflect the personality of those who live in them, creating unique environments that combine comfort, creativity and practical solutions, always with the aim of offering spaces that inspire and improve the quality of life.

L'architecte Yevheniia Sytnik a fondé son studio en 2016 dans le but de donner vie à des projets de conception qui fusionnent esthétique et fonctionnalité. Après avoir suivi une formation à l'Académie de la construction et acquis de l'expérience dans un cabinet d'architectes à Kyiv, elle a décidé de créer son propre espace pour concrétiser sa vision. Depuis sa création, elle a su consolider une équipe de professionnels qui partagent son approche innovante et s'adaptent aux besoins de chaque client. La philosophie du studio vise à concevoir des intérieurs qui reflètent la personnalité de ceux qui y vivent, en créant des environnements uniques qui combinent confort, créativité et solutions pratiques, toujours dans le but d'offrir des espaces qui inspirent et améliorent la qualité de vie.

Die Architektin Yevheniia Sytnik gründete ihr Studio im Jahr 2016 mit dem Ziel, Designprojekte zu realisieren, die Ästhetik und Funktionalität miteinander verbinden. Nach ihrer Ausbildung an der Akademie für Bauwesen und ersten Berufserfahrungen in einem Architekturbüro in Kyjiw entschied sie sich, einen eigenen Raum zu schaffen, um ihre Vision umzusetzen. Seit der Gründung ist es ihr gelungen, ein Team von Fachleuten aufzubauen, das ihren innovativen Ansatz teilt und sich flexibel an die Bedürfnisse jedes einzelnen Kunden anpasst. Die Philosophie des Studios besteht darin, Innenräume zu gestalten, die die Persönlichkeit der Menschen widerspiegeln, die sie bewohnen – einzigartige Umgebungen, die Komfort, Kreativität und praxisorientierte Lösungen vereinen, stets mit dem Anspruch, inspirierende Räume zu schaffen, die die Lebensqualität verbessern.

La arquitecta Yevheniia Sytnik fundó su estudio en 2016 con el propósito de dar vida a proyectos de diseño que fusionan estética y funcionalidad. Tras formarse en la Academia de Construcción y adquirir experiencia en una firma de arquitectura en Kyiv, decidió crear un espacio propio para materializar su visión. Desde sus inicios, ha logrado consolidar un equipo de profesionales que comparten su enfoque innovador y adaptado a las necesidades de cada cliente. La filosofía del estudio busca diseñar interiores que reflejan la personalidad de quienes los habitan, creando ambientes únicos que combinan confort, creatividad y soluciones prácticas, siempre con el objetivo de ofrecer espacios que inspiren y mejoren la calidad de vida.

P. 84 < COLOR & LIGHT IN BUSSUM

EVEN ELEVEN INTERIOR DESIGN STUDIO

MICHELLE JAGER VAN'T HOF
PIETER JAGER

BUSSUM, THE NETHERLANDS
eveneleven.nl

Even Eleven is an interior design studio based in Bussum, founded by Michelle Jager van't Hof and Pieter Jager. Their approach, rooted in modern maximalism, blends clean lines and playful forms with contemporary designs and vintage classics. With a portfolio spanning a wide range of residential projects—from mansions to modern penthouses—the studio is known for its ability to create unique spaces by harmoniously integrating diverse elements, always seeking innovation and personal style in every project.

Even Eleven est un studio de design d'intérieur basé à Bussum, fondé par Michelle Jager van't Hof et Pieter Jager. Leur approche, basée sur le maximalisme moderne, combine des lignes épurées et des formes ludiques avec des designs contemporains et classiques. Avec une expérience qui comprend une grande variété de projets résidentiels, des manoirs aux penthouses modernes, le studio se distingue par sa capacité à créer des espaces uniques en intégrant divers éléments de manière harmonieuse, en recherchant toujours l'innovation et le style personnel dans chaque projet.

Even Eleven ist ein Interior-Design-Studio mit Sitz in Bussum, gegründet von Michelle Jager van't Hof und Pieter Jager. Ihr Ansatz, geprägt vom modernen Maximalismus, vereint klare Linien und verspielte Formen mit zeitgenössischem Design und klassischen Vintage-Elementen. Mit einem vielseitigen Portfolio, das von Herrenhäusern bis hin zu modernen Penthouses reicht, zeichnet sich das Studio durch seine Fähigkeit aus, einzigartige Räume zu schaffen. Durch die harmonische Integration verschiedener Stilelemente gelingt es ihnen, in jedem Projekt Innovation und persönliche Ästhetik miteinander zu verbinden.

Even Eleven es un estudio de diseño de interiores con sede en Bussum, fundado por Michelle Jager van't Hof y Pieter Jager. Su enfoque, basado en el maximalismo moderno, combina líneas limpias y formas lúdicas con diseños contemporáneos, clásicos vintage. Con una trayectoria que incluye una amplia variedad de proyectos residenciales, desde mansiones hasta áticos modernos, el estudio se destaca por su habilidad para crear espacios únicos al integrar diversos elementos de manera armónica, buscando siempre la innovación y el estilo personal en cada proyecto.

P. 92 < FLEMINGTON HOUSE

LISA BREEZE, ARCHITECTURE AND INTERIORS

LISA BREEZE

MELBOURNE, AUSTRALIA
lisabreeze.com.au

Lisa Breeze is an architect specialising in residential design. The Melbourne-based firm's work ranges from new builds to renovations and extensions of heritage homes. Her approach combines sustainability, functionality and aesthetics, with a focus on creating living spaces that endure over time.
The architect distinguishes herself through the use of simple materials to provide texture and refined forms with the aim of generating spatial dynamism. Her design process is thoughtful and adaptable, structured yet flexible, ensuring a fluid and enriching experience. The studio's aim in all its work is to create homes that not only respond to today's needs, but are also treasured for generations to come.

Lisa Breeze est une architecte spécialisée dans la conception résidentielle. Le travail du cabinet basé à Melbourne va des nouvelles constructions aux rénovations et extensions de maisons patrimoniales. Son approche combine la durabilité, la fonctionnalité et l'esthétique, en mettant l'accent sur la création d'espaces de vie qui durent dans le temps.
L'architecte est connue pour son utilisation de matériaux simples pour donner de la texture et des formes raffinées dans le but de générer un dynamisme spatial. Son processus de conception est réfléchi et adaptable, structuré mais flexible, ce qui garantit une expérience fluide et enrichissante. L'objectif du studio dans tout son travail est de créer des maisons qui non seulement répondent aux besoins d'aujourd'hui, mais qui seront également chéries par les générations à venir.

Lisa Breeze ist eine Architektin, die sich auf die Gestaltung von Wohnhäusern spezialisiert hat. Die Arbeit des in Melbourne ansässigen Büros reicht von Neubauten bis hin zu Renovierungen und Erweiterungen von historischen Häusern. Ihr Ansatz verbindet Nachhaltigkeit, Funktionalität und Ästhetik mit dem Ziel, Lebensräume zu schaffen, die über die Zeit Bestand haben.
Die Architektin ist bekannt für die Verwendung einfacher Materialien, die Textur und raffinierte Formen schaffen, um eine räumliche Dynamik zu erzeugen. Ihr Entwurfsprozess ist durchdacht und anpassungsfähig, strukturiert und doch flexibel, um eine fließende und bereichernde Erfahrung zu gewährleisten. Das Ziel des Studios ist es, Häuser zu schaffen, die nicht nur den heutigen Bedürfnissen entsprechen, sondern auch für kommende Generationen erhalten bleiben.

Lisa Breeze es una arquitecta especializada en diseño residencial. Los trabajos de su firma con sede en Melbourne abarcan desde nuevas construcciones hasta renovaciones y ampliaciones de viviendas patrimoniales. Su enfoque combina sostenibilidad, funcionalidad y estética, orientado hacia la creación de espacios habitables que perduran en el tiempo.
La arquitecta se distingue por el uso de materiales simples para aportar textura y formas depuradas con el objetivo de generar dinamismo espacial. Su proceso de diseño es reflexivo y adaptable, estructurado pero flexible, asegurando una experiencia fluida y enriquecedora. El objetivo del estudio en todos sus trabajos es crear viviendas que no solo respondan a las necesidades actuales, sino que también sean atesorados por generaciones.

P. 100 < SLOANE COURT WEST APARTMENT

LEHLO INTERIORS

CLEME DE GRIVEL

LONDON, UNITED KINGDOM
lehlointeriors.com

Founded in London in 2009 by Cleme de Grivel, Lehlo Interiors specialises in high-end residential and commercial projects. Of Parisian origin with Spanish and Mauritian roots, the designer brings her multicultural approach to creating spaces that are balanced, contemporary and full of character. Attention to detail and the use of carefully selected materials, textures and patterns define each intervention. From bespoke furniture design to collaboration with artisans, each project is developed as a personalised and collaborative process. Their portfolio spans UK and international work, combining functionality, elegance and comfort.

Fondé à Londres en 2009 par Cleme de Grivel, Lehlo Interiors est spécialisé dans les projets résidentiels et commerciaux haut de gamme. D'origine parisienne avec des racines espagnoles et mauriciennes, la designer apporte son approche multiculturelle à la création d'espaces équilibrés, contemporains et pleins de caractère. L'attention portée aux détails et l'utilisation de matériaux, de textures et de motifs soigneusement sélectionnés définissent chaque intervention. De la conception de meubles sur mesure à la collaboration avec des artisans, chaque projet est développé dans le cadre d'un processus personnalisé et collaboratif. Leur portefeuille comprend des travaux britanniques et internationaux, alliant fonctionnalité, élégance et confort.

Lehlo Interiors wurde 2009 von Cleme de Grivel in London gegründet und hat sich auf hochwertige Wohn- und Gewerbeprojekte spezialisiert. Die aus Paris stammende Designerin mit spanischen und mauritischen Wurzeln bringt ihren multikulturellen Ansatz ein, um Räume zu schaffen, die ausgewogen, zeitgemäß und voller Charakter sind. Die Liebe zum Detail und die Verwendung sorgfältig ausgewählter Materialien, Texturen und Muster prägen jede Intervention. Vom maßgeschneiderten Möbeldesign bis zur Zusammenarbeit mit Kunsthandwerkern wird jedes Projekt in einem persönlichen und gemeinschaftlichen Prozess entwickelt. Ihr Portfolio umfasst britische und internationale Arbeiten, die Funktionalität, Eleganz und Komfort miteinander verbinden.

Fundado en Londres en 2009 por Cleme de Grivel, Lehlo Interiors, se especializa en proyectos residenciales y comerciales de alta gama. De origen parisino con raíces españolas y mauricianas, la diseñadora aporta su enfoque multicultural en la creación de espacios equilibrados, contemporáneos y llenos de carácter. La atención al detalle y el uso de materiales, texturas y patrones cuidadosamente seleccionados definen cada intervención. Desde el diseño de mobiliario a medida hasta la colaboración con artesanos, cada proyecto se desarrolla como un proceso personalizado y colaborativo. Su portafolio abarca trabajos en el Reino Unido e internacionales, combinando funcionalidad, elegancia y confort.

P. 110 < APPARTEMENT MERVEILLEUX

© Laurence Revol

LUCIE SOCRATE STUDIO

LUCIE SOCRATE

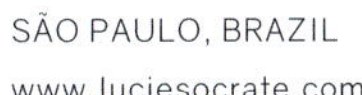
SÃO PAULO, BRAZIL
www.luciesocrate.com

Lucie Socrate is an interior designer, born in Paris and based in São Paulo, Brazil. After a decade as a finance director at Chanel, immersed in an environment where talent and craftsmanship were central, the designer chose to reinvent herself and pursue interior design. She trained at GRETA Création, Design et Métiers d'Art in Boulle, thus reestablishing her link with creativity.
In 2022 she founded her own studio, specialising in residential projects. Her interiors are characterised by spatial fluidity, the use of natural materials and the combination of vintage furniture with bold colour palettes. The studio collaborates with independent brands, developing objects and decorative pieces.

Lucie Socrate est une architecte d'intérieur née à Paris et installée à São Paulo, au Brésil. Après une décennie en tant que directrice financière chez Chanel, immergée dans un environnement où le talent et l'artisanat étaient essentiels, la designer a décidé de se réinventer et de se consacrer au design d'intérieur. Elle se forme au GRETA Création, Design et Métiers d'Art à Boulle, renouant ainsi avec la créativité.
En 2022, elle fonde son propre studio, spécialisé dans les projets résidentiels. Ses intérieurs se caractérisent par la fluidité spatiale, l'utilisation de matériaux naturels et l'association de mobilier vintage à des palettes de couleurs audacieuses. Le studio collabore avec des marques indépendantes, développant des objets et des pièces de décoration.

Lucie Socrate ist eine Innenarchitektin, die in Paris geboren wurde und in São Paulo, Brasilien, lebt. Nach einem Jahrzehnt als Finanzdirektorin bei Chanel, eingebettet in ein Umfeld, in dem Talent und Handwerkskunst essenziell waren, entschied sich die Designerin, sich neu zu erfinden und sich der Innenarchitektur zu widmen. Sie absolviert eine Ausbildung an der GRETA Création, Design et Métiers d'Art in Boulle und stellt so ihre Verbindung zur Kreativität wieder her.
Im Jahr 2022 gründete er sein eigenes Studio, das sich auf Wohnprojekte spezialisiert hat. Seine Interieurs zeichnen sich durch eine fließende Raumgestaltung, die Verwendung natürlicher Materialien und die Kombination von Vintage-Möbeln mit kräftigen Farbpaletten aus. Das Studio arbeitet mit unabhängigen Marken zusammen und entwickelt Objekte und Dekorationsgegenstände.

Lucie Socrate es diseñadora de interiores, nacida en París y afincada en São Paulo, Brasil. Tras una década como directora financiera en Chanel, inmersa en un entorno donde el talento y la artesanía eran fundamentales, la diseñadora decidió reinventarse y dedicarse al diseño de interiores. Se formó en GRETA Création, Design et Métiers d'Art en Boulle, retomando así su vínculo con la creatividad.
En 2022 fundó su propio estudio, especializado en proyectos residenciales. Sus interiores se caracterizan por la fluidez espacial, el uso de materiales naturales y la combinación de mobiliario vintage con paletas cromáticas audaces. El estudio colabora con marcas independientes, desarrollando objetos y piezas decorativas.

P. 118 < NEDU

MARTÍN PELÁEZ ESTUDIO

FRANCISCO PELÁEZ
AINHOA MARTÍN

MADRID, SPAIN
martin-pelaez.es

Founded in 2016 in Madrid by Francisco Peláez and Ainhoa Martín, Martín Peláez Estudio is an architecture and design firm that undertakes projects of various scales, from buildings to interior design, retail, installations, and environmental graphics. Francisco Peláez, an architect with international training, has worked in renowned firms and led large-scale projects. Ainhoa Martín, an architect and graphic designer, has worked in distinguished studios, specializing in interior design, retail, and environmental graphic design. The studio is characterized by a simple yet powerful language, always focused on the essence of the concept.

Gegründet 2016 in Madrid von Francisco Peláez und Ainhoa Martín, ist Martín Peláez Estudio ein Architektur- und Designbüro, das Projekte in verschiedenen Dimensionen realisiert, von Gebäuden bis hin zu Innenarchitektur, Einzelhandel, Installationen und Umweltgrafik. Francisco Peláez, ein Architekt mit internationaler Ausbildung, hat in renommierten Büros gearbeitet und große Projekte geleitet. Ainhoa Martín, Architektin und Grafikdesignerin, hat sich auf Innenarchitektur, Einzelhandel und Umweltgrafik spezialisiert. Das Studio zeichnet sich durch eine klare und kraftvolle Sprache aus, die stets auf das Wesentliche des Konzepts fokussiert ist.

Fondé en 2016 à Madrid par Francisco Peláez et Ainhoa Martín, Martín Peláez Estudio est un cabinet d'architecture et de design qui couvre des projets de différentes échelles, des bâtiments au design d'intérieur, en passant par le commerce de détail, les installations et le graphisme environnemental. Francisco Peláez, architecte de formation internationale, a travaillé dans plusieurs cabinets renommés et dirigé des projets de grande envergure. Ainhoa Martín, architecte et graphiste, a travaillé dans des studios de premier plan, se spécialisant dans l'aménagement intérieur, la vente au détail et le graphisme environnemental. Le studio se caractérise par un langage simple et énergique, toujours axé sur l'essence du concept.

Fundado en 2016 en Madrid por Francisco Peláez y Ainhoa Martín, Martín Peláez Estudio, es una firma de arquitectura y diseño que abarca proyectos de diversas escalas, desde edificios hasta interiorismo, retail, instalaciones y gráfica ambiental. Francisco Peláez, arquitecto con una formación internacional, ha trabajado en diversas firmas de renombre y liderado proyectos de gran envergadura. Ainhoa Martín, arquitecta y diseñadora gráfica, ha trabajado en estudios destacados, especializándose en interiorismo, retail y diseño gráfico ambiental. El estudio se caracteriza por un lenguaje simple y contundente, siempre enfocado en la esencia del concepto.

P. 126 < CASA COA

MAYE ESTUDIO

MAYE RUIZ

SAN MIGUEL DE ALLENDE, MEXICO
maye.mx

Maye Estudio is an interdisciplinary design firm that fuses tradition and innovation in collaborative projects. Founded by Mayela Ruiz, a graduate in Environmental Design with extensive experience in interior design, the firm is distinguished by its creative and collaborative approach. The Guanajuato-born designer has worked with firms such as Mestiz and Atelier TBD. In addition to leading her own studio, she is an academic and has taught courses, conferences and workshops at institutions such as the Universidad Iberoamericana, the Tecnológico de Monterrey and the Centro de Diseño, Cine y TV, sharing her knowledge and experience with new generations of designers.

Maye Estudio est un cabinet de design interdisciplinaire qui fusionne tradition et innovation dans des projets collaboratifs. Fondée par Mayela Ruiz, diplômée en design environnemental et dotée d'une vaste expérience en design d'intérieur, l'entreprise se distingue par son approche créative et collaborative. Cette designer originaire de Guanajuato a travaillé avec des entreprises telles que Mestiz et Atelier TBD. En plus de diriger son propre studio, elle est universitaire et a donné des cours, des conférences et des ateliers dans des institutions telles que l'Universidad Iberoamericana, le Tecnológico de Monterrey et le Centro de Diseño, Cine y TV, partageant ses connaissances et son expérience avec de nouvelles générations de designers.

Maye Estudio ist ein interdisziplinäres Designbüro, das Tradition und Innovation in gemeinsamen Projekten miteinander verbindet. Gegründet von Mayela Ruiz, einer Absolventin des Studiengangs Umweltdesign mit umfassender Erfahrung in der Innenarchitektur, zeichnet sich das Unternehmen durch seinen kreativen und kooperativen Ansatz aus. Die in Guanajuato geborene Designerin hat mit Firmen wie Mestiz und Atelier TBD zusammengearbeitet. Sie leitet nicht nur ihr eigenes Studio, sondern ist auch Akademikerin und hat Kurse, Konferenzen und Workshops an Institutionen wie der Universidad Iberoamericana, dem Tecnológico de Monterrey und dem Centro de Diseño, Cine y TV abgehalten, wo sie ihr Wissen und ihre Erfahrung an neue Generationen von Designern weitergibt.

Maye Estudio es una firma de diseño interdisciplinario que fusiona tradición e innovación en proyectos colaborativos. Fundada por Mayela Ruiz, licenciada en Diseño Ambiental con una amplia experiencia en diseño de interiores, la firma se distingue por su enfoque creativo y colaborativo. La diseñadora originaria de Guanajuato, ha trabajado con firmas como Mestiz y Atelier TBD. Además de liderar su propio estudio, es académica y ha impartido cursos, conferencias y talleres en instituciones como la Universidad Iberoamericana, el Tecnológico de Monterrey y el Centro de Diseño, Cine y TV, compartiendo su conocimiento y experiencia con nuevas generaciones de diseñadores.

P. 134 < LA TORRE

MIRTA OTTAVIANI

MIRTA OTTAVIANI

ROME, ITALY
mirtaottaviani.com

Mirta Ottaviani is an architect and interior designer based in Rome, specializing in residential and commercial renovations. Her design philosophy is based on an immersive approach, where architecture and design form a unique and cohesive vision. In her mother's creative workshop, surrounded by fabrics and stones, she learned the art of composition, harmonizing shapes, colors, and materials. After completing her Architecture degree at Roma Tre University with a thesis at the École Nationale Supérieure d'Architecture in Lyon, she worked in several design studios in Italy and France before founding her own studio in 2021.

Mirta Ottaviani est une architecte et décoratrice d'intérieur basée à Rome, spécialisée dans les rénovations résidentielles et commerciales. Sa philosophie en matière de design repose sur une approche immersive, où l'architecture et le design ne forment qu'une seule et même vision. Dans l'atelier créatif de sa mère, entourée de tissus et de pierres, elle a appris l'art de la composition, en harmonisant les formes, les couleurs et les matériaux. Après avoir obtenu son diplôme d'architecture à l'université Roma Tre et une thèse à l'École nationale supérieure d'architecture de Lyon, l'architecte a travaillé dans divers bureaux d'études en Italie et en France avant de fonder son propre studio en 2021.

Mirta Ottaviani ist eine in Rom ansässige Architektin und Innenarchitektin, spezialisiert auf Wohn- und Gewerberenovierungen. Ihr Designansatz ist immersiv und betrachtet Architektur und Gestaltung als eine einheitliche Vision. In der Kreativwerkstatt ihrer Mutter, umgeben von Stoffen und Steinen, lernte sie das Zusammenspiel von Formen, Farben und Materialien. Nach ihrem Architekturstudium an der Universität Roma Tre mit einer Abschlussarbeit an der École Nationale Supérieure d'Architecture in Lyon arbeitete sie in mehreren Designstudios in Italien und Frankreich, bevor sie 2021 ihr eigenes Studio gründete.

Mirta Ottaviani es arquitecta y diseñadora de interiores con sede en Roma, especializada en renovaciones residenciales y comerciales. Su filosofía de diseño se basa en un enfoque inmersivo, con la arquitectura y el diseño como una visión única y cohesionada. En el taller creativo de su madre, rodeada de telas y piedras, aprendió el arte de la composición, armonizando formas, colores y materiales. Tras completar su licenciatura en Arquitectura en la Universidad Roma Tre con una tesis en la École Nationale Supérieure d'Architecture de Lyon, la arquitecta trabajó en varios estudios de diseño en Italia y Francia antes de fundar su propio estudio en 2021.

P. 144 < TWO LOST KIDS APARTMENT

MOCA ARQUITETURA

ANA SIKORSKI
KATIA AZEVEDO

CURITIBA, BRAZIL
moca.life

Founded by architects Ana Sikorski and Katia Azevedo, Moca Arquitetura develops architectural and interior design projects for both commercial and residential spaces. Based in Curitiba, the studio approaches each project with meticulous attention to detail, prioritizing the harmony between spaces and their inhabitants.
More than just aesthetics, their work aims to create atmospheres that evoke memories and reinforce people's emotional connection with their surroundings. Through design, they transform spaces into livable settings with unique identities, reflecting the history and personality of those who occupy them.

Fondé par les architectes Ana Sikorski et Katia Azevedo, Moca Arquitetura développe des projets d'architecture et de design d'intérieur pour des espaces commerciaux et résidentiels. Basé à Curitiba, le studio aborde chaque projet avec une approche détaillée, donnant la priorité à l'harmonie entre les espaces et ceux qui les habitent.
Plus qu'une question d'esthétique, le travail du studio cherche à générer des atmosphères qui éveillent des souvenirs et renforcent la relation émotionnelle des gens avec leur environnement. Par le biais du design, il cherche à transformer les espaces en scénarios habitables dotés d'une identité propre, reflétant l'histoire et la personnalité de ceux qui les occupent.

Gegründet von den Architektinnen Ana Sikorski und Katia Azevedo, entwickelt Moca Arquitetura Projekte für Architektur und Interior Design in Wohn- und Geschäftsräumen. Mit Sitz in Curitiba verfolgt das Studio einen detaillierten Ansatz, der die Harmonie zwischen Räumen und ihren Bewohnern priorisiert.
Mehr als eine bloße Ästhetik geht es darum, Atmosphären zu schaffen, die Erinnerungen wecken und die emotionale Verbindung der Menschen zu ihrem Umfeld stärken. Ihr Design verwandelt Räume in lebendige Bühnen mit einzigartiger Identität, die die Geschichte und Persönlichkeit ihrer Bewohner widerspiegeln.

Fundado por las arquitectas Ana Sikorski y Katia Azevedo, Moca Arquitetura desarrolla proyectos arquitectónicos y de diseño de interiores para espacios comerciales y residenciales. Con sede en Curitiba, el estudio aborda cada proyecto con un enfoque detallado, priorizando la armonía entre los espacios y quienes los habitan.
Más que una cuestión estética, el trabajo del estudio busca generar atmósferas que despierten memorias y refuercen la relación emocional de las personas con su entorno. A través del diseño, busca transformar espacios en escenarios habitables con identidad propia, reflejando la historia y personalidad de quienes los ocupan.

P. 150 < FAMILY HOUSE IN MAARSSEN

NOX STUDIO INTERIORS

ANNE VAN HEUGTEN

AMERSFOORT, THE NETHERLANDS
noxstudiointeriors.nl

Nox Studio Interiors is an interior design firm established in 2020 by Anne van Heugten, specializing in creating exclusive, functional, and sophisticated concepts for residential and commercial spaces. With a strong background in fashion, its founder brings a unique vision that blends aesthetics and functionality into every project. The studio's approach focuses on reflecting the client's identity and needs, using luxury materials, refined details, and a carefully chosen color palette, always seeking a balance between design and comfort.
In 2022, the studio was awarded the De Interieur Club's Interior Talent of 2022 award, a recognition of its innovative approach and ability to transform spaces into inspiring and personalized environments.

Nox Studio Interiors est un cabinet de design d'intérieur fondé en 2020 par Anne van Heugten, spécialisé dans la création de concepts exclusifs, fonctionnels et sophistiqués pour les résidences et les espaces commerciaux. Avec une solide expérience dans le monde de la mode, sa fondatrice apporte une vision unique qui fusionne esthétique et fonctionnalité dans chaque projet. L'approche du studio est axée sur la mise en valeur de l'identité et des besoins du client, en utilisant des matériaux luxueux, des détails raffinés et une palette de couleurs soigneusement sélectionnée, cherchant toujours un équilibre entre design et confort.
En 2022, le studio a reçu le prix De Interieur Club - Interior Talent of 2022, une reconnaissance de son approche innovante et de sa capacité à transformer les espaces en environnements inspirants et personnalisés.

Nox Studio Interiors ist ein Interior-Design-Studio, das 2020 von Anne van Heugten gegründet wurde und sich auf die Entwicklung exklusiver, funktionaler und anspruchsvoller Konzepte für Wohn- und Geschäftsräume spezialisiert hat. Mit einem soliden Hintergrund in der Modebranche bringt die Gründerin eine einzigartige Vision mit, die Ästhetik und Funktionalität in jedem Projekt vereint. Der Fokus des Studios liegt darauf, die Identität und die Bedürfnisse der Kunden widerzuspiegeln, indem luxuriöse Materialien, raffinierte Details und eine sorgfältig ausgewählte Farbpalette verwendet werden – stets mit dem Ziel, ein Gleichgewicht zwischen Design und Komfort zu schaffen.
Im Jahr 2022 wurde das Studio mit dem De Interieur Club Award als „Interior Talent of 2022" ausgezeichnet – eine Anerkennung für seinen innovativen Ansatz und seine Fähigkeit, Räume in inspirierende und personalisierte Umgebungen zu verwandeln.

Nox Studio Interiors es una firma de diseño de interiores creado en 2020, por Anne van Heugten, especializada en crear conceptos exclusivos, funcionales y sofisticados para viviendas y espacios comerciales. Con un sólido trasfondo en el mundo de la moda, su fundadora aporta una visión única que fusiona estética y funcionalidad en cada proyecto. El enfoque del estudio se centra en reflejar la identidad y las necesidades del cliente, utilizando materiales de lujo, detalles refinados y una paleta de colores cuidadosamente seleccionada, siempre buscando un equilibrio entre diseño y confort.
En 2022, el estudio fue galardonado con el premio De Interieur Club a Interior Talent of 2022, un reconocimiento a su enfoque innovador y su capacidad para transformar los espacios en ambientes inspiradores y personalizados.

P. 158 < CHEERFUL COLORS IN BYDGOSZCZ

PRACOWNIA DUŻY POKÓJ

SYLWIA LASHMANN
MAREK LEWANDOWSKI

BYDGOSZCZ, POLAND
pracowniadp.pl

Led by Sylwia Lashmann and Marek Lewandowski, Pracownia Duży Pokój is a design studio that blends Fine Arts training with an analytical and creative perspective. Their approach is rooted in material exploration, a dialogue between tradition and modernity, and the search for customized solutions for every space.
Inspired by art, craftsmanship, and contemporary design, the designers develop residential and commercial projects with a strong focus on detail and functionality. In addition to interior design, they offer guidance in selecting images and graphics that best complement each space, ensuring a harmonious visual composition. They oversee every stage of the process to guarantee coherence and quality.

Geleitet von Sylwia Lashmann und Marek Lewandowski, verbindet das Designstudio Pracownia Duży Pokój eine Ausbildung in Bildender Kunst mit einem analytischen und kreativen Ansatz. Ihr Fokus liegt auf der Erforschung von Materialien, dem Dialog zwischen Tradition und Moderne sowie maßgeschneiderten Lösungen für jeden Raum.
Inspiriert von Kunst, Handwerk und zeitgenössischem Design entwerfen sie sowohl Wohn- als auch Gewerbeprojekte mit Liebe zum Detail und Funktionalität. Neben Innenarchitektur beraten sie auch bei der Auswahl von Bildern und Grafiken, um eine harmonische visuelle Komposition zu gewährleisten. Sie begleiten jede Phase des Prozesses, um Kohärenz und höchste Qualität sicherzustellen.

Dirigé par Sylwia Lashmann et Marek Lewandowski, Pracownia Duży Pokój est un studio de design qui allie une formation en beaux-arts à un œil analytique et créatif. Leur approche est basée sur l'exploration des matériaux, le dialogue entre tradition et modernité, et la recherche de solutions personnalisées pour chaque espace.
Inspirés par l'art, l'artisanat et le design contemporain, les designers développent des projets résidentiels et commerciaux avec le souci du détail et de la fonctionnalité. Outre la décoration d'intérieur, ils conseillent la sélection d'images et de graphiques adaptés à chaque environnement, garantissant ainsi une composition visuelle harmonieuse. Ils supervisent chaque étape du processus afin de garantir la cohérence et la qualité.

Dirigido por Sylwia Lashmann y Marek Lewandowski, Pracownia Duży Pokój es un estudio de diseño que combina la formación en Bellas Artes con una mirada analítica y creativa. Su enfoque se basa en la exploración de materiales, el diálogo entre tradición y modernidad, y la búsqueda de soluciones personalizadas para cada espacio.
Inspirados por el arte, la artesanía y el diseño contemporáneo, los diseñadores desarrollan proyectos residenciales y comerciales con atención al detalle y a la funcionalidad. Además del diseño interior, asesoran en la selección de imágenes y gráficos adecuados para cada ambiente, asegurando una composición visual armónica. Supervisan cada fase del proceso para garantizar coherencia y calidad.

P. 166 < JEAN-JACQUES ROUSSEAU

ROOM SERVICE STUDIO

VALENTINE RICHARDSON

LILLE, FRANCE
roomservicestudio.fr

Valentine Richardson is an interior decorator, set designer, and founder of Room Service Studio. Her experience allows her to shift between different roles, skillfully handling bold color palettes to create unique atmospheres. She works on both professional projects—such as restaurants, guest houses, and co-living spaces—and for private clients looking to immerse themselves in her creative universe. Her approach combines functionality and aesthetics, offering personalized solutions that balance comfort, creativity, and modern design. Her work stands out for its ability to transform each space into a unique, thoughtfully designed environment.

Valentine Richardson est décoratrice d'intérieur, scénographe et fondatrice de Room Service Studio. Son expérience lui permet d'alterner entre différents rôles, maniant habilement des palettes de couleurs audacieuses pour créer des environnements uniques. Elle travaille aussi bien pour des projets professionnels, tels que des restaurants, des maisons d'hôtes et des espaces de cohabitation, que pour des clients privés désireux de plonger dans son univers créatif. Son approche combine fonctionnalité et esthétique, offrant des solutions personnalisées qui concilient confort, créativité et design moderne. Son travail se distingue par sa capacité à transformer chaque espace en un lieu unique, pensé et conçu sur mesure.

Valentine Richardson ist Innenarchitektin, Set-Designerin und Gründerin von Room Service Studio. Ihre Erfahrung ermöglicht es ihr, flexibel zwischen verschiedenen Rollen zu wechseln und mit mutigen Farbpaletten einzigartige Atmosphären zu schaffen. Sie arbeitet sowohl für professionelle Projekte – darunter Restaurants, Gästehäuser und Co-Living-Spaces – als auch für Privatkunden, die in ihr kreatives Universum eintauchen möchten. Ihr Ansatz verbindet Funktionalität mit Ästhetik und bietet maßgeschneiderte Lösungen, die Komfort, Kreativität und modernes Design vereinen. Ihre Arbeit zeichnet sich durch die Fähigkeit aus, jeden Raum in einen einzigartigen, durchdachten und maßgeschneiderten Ort zu verwandeln.

Valentine Richardson es decoradora de interiores, set designer y fundadora de Room Service Studio. Su experiencia le permite alternar entre diferentes roles, manejando con destreza paletas de colores audaces para crear ambientes únicos. Trabaja tanto para proyectos profesionales, como restaurantes, casas de huéspedes y espacios de co-living, como para clientes particulares que buscan adentrarse en su universo creativo. Su enfoque combina funcionalidad y estética, ofreciendo soluciones personalizadas que equilibran confort, creatividad y diseño moderno. Su trabajo se distingue por la capacidad de transformar cada espacio en un lugar único, pensado y diseñado a medida.

P. 172 < GILLIS RESIDENCE

STUDIO 34 SOUTH

CHECHI VALENTINE

AMSTERDAM, THE NETHERLANDS
studio34south.com

Studio 34 South was founded in 2017 by two designers from Buenos Aires and Sydney, connected by the 34th parallel south. Today, the studio is led from Amsterdam by Chechi Valentine, who brings her personal approach and passion for pure design and effective problem-solving. With a background in product design, furniture, and interior architecture, she has led projects across the retail, hospitality, and residential sectors throughout Europe. Her Latin warmth, combined with refined technical skills, translates into functional and innovative designs that always maintain a balance between aesthetics and practicality.

Studio 34 South a été fondé en 2017 avec la vision commune de deux designers de Buenos Aires et Sydney, reliés par le 34e parallèle sud. Actuellement, Chechi Valentine dirige le studio depuis Amsterdam, apportant son approche personnelle et sa passion pour le design pur et la résolution efficace des problèmes. Forte d'une expérience dans le design de produits, le mobilier et l'architecture d'intérieur, elle a dirigé des projets dans les secteurs de la vente au détail, de l'hôtellerie et de l'habitat dans toute l'Europe. Sa chaleur latine, associée à des compétences raffinées, se traduit par un travail fonctionnel et innovant, toujours avec une approche esthétique et fonctionnelle.

Studio 34 South wurde 2017 mit einer gemeinsamen Vision von zwei Designern aus Buenos Aires und Sydney gegründet, die durch den 34. südlichen Breitengrad verbunden sind. Heute wird das Studio von Chechi Valentine in Amsterdam geleitet, die ihre persönliche Handschrift und Leidenschaft für durchdachtes Design sowie funktionale Lösungen einbringt.
Mit Erfahrung in Produkt-, Möbel- und Innenarchitektur hat sie Projekte in den Bereichen Einzelhandel, Gastgewerbe und Wohnungsbau in ganz Europa geleitet. Ihr lateinamerikanisches Temperament gepaart mit raffiniertem Können zeigt sich in funktionalen und innovativen Designs, die stets eine ästhetische und praktische Balance wahren.

El Studio 34 South se fundó en 2017 con la visión compartida de dos diseñadores de Buenos Aires y Sídney, conectados por el paralelo 34° sur. Actualmente, Chechi Valentine lidera el estudio desde Ámsterdam, aportando su enfoque personal y pasión por el diseño puro y la resolución efectiva de problemas. Con experiencia en diseño de productos, mobiliario y arquitectura de interiores, ha dirigido proyectos en sectores minorista, hostelero y residencial en toda Europa. Su calidez latina, combinada con habilidades refinadas, se traduce en trabajos funcionales e innovadores, siempre con un enfoque estético y funcional.

P. 180 < CHROMA PENTHOUSE

STUDIO BOSKO

KASIA KRONBERGER

BERLIN, GERMANY
bosko.studio

Studio Bosko is an AD100 interior design and architecture studio based in Berlin and Warsaw, renowned for created spaces filled with character. At the helm is Kasia Kronberger, an interior designer certified in trend forecasting and background in fashion. Her international experience - gained in London, Florence, Barcelona and Brussels - brings a global outlook to projects that layer character, culture and craftsmanship.
The studio works with clients ranging from creative entrepreneurs to executives and their families, translating their vision into carefully curated interiors combining functionality with sophistication. Its project span Germany, Poland and beyond, consolidating an identity marked by layered sensibility and attention to detail.

Basé à Berlin et à Varsovie, Studio Bosko est une agence d'architecture et de design d'intérieur figurant sur la liste AD100, réputée pour la création d'espaces à forte identité. À sa tête, Kasia Kronberger, designer d'intérieur certifiée en analyse des tendances et issue du monde de la mode. Son expérience internationale – acquise à Londres, Florence, Barcelone et Bruxelles – insuffle une vision globale à des projets où convergent caractère, culture et savoir-faire artisanal.
Le studio collabore avec une clientèle variée, allant des entrepreneurs créatifs aux cadres dirigeants et à leurs familles, traduisant leur vision en intérieurs méticuleusement conçus, où la fonctionnalité se fond dans la sophistication. Ses projets s'étendent en Allemagne, en Pologne et au-delà, affirmant une identité marquée par une sensibilité stratifiée et une attention minutieuse aux détails.

Studio Bosko ist ein AD100-Innenarchitekturbüro mit Sitz in Berlin und Warschau, das für die Gestaltung von Räumen mit Charakter bekannt ist. An der Spitze steht Kasia Kronberger, eine Innenarchitektin mit einem Zertifikat für Trendprognosen und einem Hintergrund in der Modebranche. Ihre internationale Erfahrung, die sie in London, Florenz, Barcelona und Brüssel gesammelt hat, bringt eine globale Perspektive in Projekte ein, die Charakter, Kultur und Handwerkskunst miteinander verbinden.
Das Studio arbeitet mit Kunden zusammen, die von kreativen Unternehmern bis hin zu Führungskräften und deren Familien reichen, und setzt deren Visionen in sorgfältig kuratierte Innenräume um, die Funktionalität mit Raffinesse verbinden. Seine Projekte erstrecken sich über Deutschland, Polen und darüber hinaus und festigen eine Identität, die von vielschichtiger Sensibilität und Liebe zum Detail geprägt ist.

Con sede en Berlín y Varsovia, Studio Bosko es una firma de arquitectura y diseño de interiores que forma parte de la lista AD100, reconocido por crear espacios con una fuerte identidad. Al frente se encuentra Kasia Kronberger, diseñadora de interiores certificada en análisis de tendencias y con una trayectoria en el mundo de la moda. Su experiencia internacional, adquirida en Londres, Florencia, Barcelona y Bruselas, aporta una visión global a proyectos donde convergen carácter, cultura y artesanía.
El estudio colabora con una clientela diversa, que abarca desde emprendedores creativos hasta altos ejecutivos y sus familias, traduciendo su visión en interiores meticulosamente concebidos, donde la funcionalidad se fusiona con la sofisticación. Sus proyectos se extienden por Alemania, Polonia y más allá, consolidando una identidad marcada por una sensibilidad estratificada y una atención minuciosa al detalle.

P. 188 < RAINBOW COUNTRY HOME IN SUSSEX

STUDIO HOLLOND

PHOEBE HOLLOND

LONDON, UNITED KINGDOM
studiohollond.com

Studio Hollond is a boutique design studio based in London, specializing in high-end interiors (both residential and commercial) and product design. Led by Phoebe Hollond—named one of House & Garden's Top 100 Interior Designers in 2023 and a Rising Star in 2022—the studio is distinguished by a style influenced by classical European architecture and refined details, with a touch of eccentricity. Before launching her own studio, Hollond was part of Beata Heuman's team. Her designs are known for striking a balance between boldness and comfort, creating timeless and unique spaces that reflect the personal stories of her clients.

Studio Hollond est un studio de design basé à Londres, spécialisé dans les intérieurs haut de gamme (résidentiels et commerciaux) et la conception de produits. Dirigé par Phoebe Hollond, qui a été nommée parmi les 100 meilleurs designers d'intérieur de House & Garden en 2023 et étoile montante en 2022, le studio se distingue par un style influencé par l'architecture européenne classique et les détails raffinés, avec une touche d'excentricité. La designer a fait partie de l'équipe de Beata Heuman avant de lancer son propre studio. Ses créations équilibrent l'audace et le confort pour créer des espaces intemporels et uniques qui reflètent l'histoire de la vie de ses clients.

Studio Hollond ist ein Boutique-Designstudio mit Sitz in London, das sich auf hochwertige Innenarchitektur (sowohl Wohn- als auch Gewerbebereiche) und Produktdesign spezialisiert hat. Geführt von Phoebe Hollond, die 2023 von House & Garden zu einer der 100 besten Innenarchitektinnen ernannt wurde und 2022 als aufstrebender Star galt, zeichnet sich das Studio durch einen Stil aus, der von klassischer europäischer Architektur und raffinierten Details geprägt ist, mit einer Prise Exzentrik. Die Designerin war Teil des Teams von Beata Heuman, bevor sie ihr eigenes Studio gründete. Ihre Entwürfe zeichnen sich durch das Gleichgewicht zwischen Kühnem und Bequemem aus, um zeitlose und einzigartige Räume zu schaffen, die die Lebensgeschichte ihrer Kunden widerspiegeln.

Studio Hollond es un estudio de diseño boutique con sede en Londres, especializado en interiores de alta gama (residenciales y comerciales) y diseño de productos. Dirigido por Phoebe Hollond, quien fue nombrada una de las 100 mejores diseñadoras de interiores por House & Garden en 2023 y una estrella emergente en 2022, el estudio se distingue por un estilo influido por la arquitectura clásica europea y detalles refinados, con un toque de excentricidad. La diseñadora formó parte del equipo de Beata Heuman antes de lanzar su propio estudio. Sus diseños destacan por el equilibrio entre lo audaz con lo cómodo, para generar espacios atemporales y únicos que reflejan la historia de vida de sus clientes.

P. 198 < BOSCO VERTICALE

STUDIO MILO

FEDERICA GOSIO
ARIANNA CROSETTA

MILAN, ITALY / LONDON, UNITED KINGDOM
studio-milo.com

Studio MILO is an interior design and architecture firm founded by Federica Gosio, interior designer, and Arianna Crosetta, architect. With offices in Milan and London, the studio combines their different experiences to create functional and thoughtful spaces. Their work is characterised by a balance between artistic vision and technical precision, offering a blend of creative ideas and practical solutions. The name Studio MILO reflects the cultural influence of both cities, fusing the elegance and craftsmanship of Milan with the innovative and cosmopolitan approach of London. Each project reflects the founders' commitment to timeless and distinctive design.

Studio MILO est un cabinet de design d'intérieur et d'architecture fondé par Federica Gosio, designer d'intérieur, et Arianna Crosetta, architecte. Avec des bureaux à Milan et à Londres, le studio combine leurs différentes expériences pour créer des espaces fonctionnels et réfléchis.
Leur travail se caractérise par un équilibre entre vision artistique et précision technique, offrant un mélange d'idées créatives et de solutions pratiques. Le nom Studio MILO reflète l'influence culturelle des deux villes, fusionnant l'élégance et le savoir-faire de Milan avec l'approche innovante et cosmopolite de Londres. Chaque projet reflète l'engagement des fondateurs en faveur d'un design intemporel et distinctif.

Studio MILO ist ein Büro für Innenarchitektur und Design, das von der Innenarchitektin Federica Gosio und der Architektin Arianna Crosetta gegründet wurde. Das Studio hat Büros in Mailand und London und kombiniert ihre unterschiedlichen Erfahrungen, um funktionale und durchdachte Räume zu schaffen.
Ihre Arbeit zeichnet sich durch ein Gleichgewicht zwischen künstlerischer Vision und technischer Präzision aus und bietet eine Mischung aus kreativen Ideen und praktischen Lösungen. Der Name Studio MILO spiegelt den kulturellen Einfluss beider Städte wider, indem er die Eleganz und Handwerkskunst Mailands mit dem innovativen und kosmopolitischen Ansatz Londons verbindet. Jedes Projekt spiegelt das Engagement der Gründer für zeitloses und unverwechselbares Design wider.

Studio MILO es una firma de diseño de interiores y arquitectura fundada por Federica Gosio, diseñadora de interiores, y Arianna Crosetta, arquitecta. Con oficinas en Milán y Londres, el estudio combina sus distintas experiencias para crear espacios funcionales y pensados en detalle.
Su trabajo se caracteriza por el equilibrio entre visión artística y precisión técnica, ofreciendo una mezcla de ideas creativas y soluciones prácticas. El nombre Studio MILO refleja la influencia cultural de ambas ciudades, fusionando la elegancia y la artesanía de Milán con el enfoque innovador y cosmopolita de Londres. Cada proyecto refleja el compromiso de las fundadoras con un diseño atemporal y distintivo.

P. 206 < MAGIC

WOWOWA ARCHITECTURE

ZOE DIACOLABRIANOS
MONIQUE WOODWARD
SCOTT WOODWARD

VICTORIA, AUSTRALIA
wowowa.com.au

Led by Monique and Scott Woodward, WOWOWA Architecture is a Melbourne-based practice specialising in residential and public projects. Their approach combines the contemporary, the playful and a grounding in innovative ideas, exploring memory and sustainability. They have won several design awards and are noted for their originality.
Monique Woodward, creative director, is a registered architect (ARBV), a Fellow of the Australian Institute of Architects (FRAIA) and a National Councillor of the Australian Institute of Architects (FRAIA). Scott Woodward is a project manager and architect with a background in fine art and sculpture. Both teach at Monash University and RMIT, promoting the impact of architecture on cities.

Dirigé par Monique et Scott Woodward, WOWOWA Architecture est un cabinet de Melbourne spécialisé dans les projets résidentiels et publics. Leur approche combine le contemporain, le ludique et un ancrage dans des idées novatrices, explorant la mémoire et la durabilité. Ils ont remporté plusieurs prix de design et sont réputés pour leur originalité.
Monique Woodward, directrice de la création, est architecte agréée (ARBV), membre de l'Australian Institute of Architects (FRAIA) et conseillère nationale de l'Australian Institute of Architects (FRAIA). Scott Woodward est chef de projet et architecte, avec une formation en beaux-arts et en sculpture. Tous deux enseignent à l'université Monash et à l'université RMIT, où ils promeuvent l'impact de l'architecture sur les villes.

WOWOWA Architecture, geleitet von Monique und Scott Woodward, ist ein in Melbourne ansässiges Büro, das sich auf Wohn- und öffentliche Projekte spezialisiert hat. Ihr Ansatz verbindet das Zeitgenössische, das Spielerische und die Verwurzelung in innovativen Ideen, die Erinnerung und Nachhaltigkeit erforschen. Sie haben mehrere Designpreise gewonnen und sind für ihre Originalität bekannt.
Monique Woodward, Kreativdirektorin, ist eingetragene Architektin (ARBV), Fellow des Australian Institute of Architects (FRAIA) und National Councillor des Australian Institute of Architects (FRAIA). Scott Woodward ist Projektmanager und Architekt mit einem Hintergrund in bildender Kunst und Bildhauerei. Beide lehren an der Monash University und am RMIT und beschäftigen sich mit dem Einfluss der Architektur auf die Städte.

Liderado por Monique y Scott Woodward, WOWOWA Architecture es un estudio con oficina en Melbourne especializado en proyectos residenciales y públicos. Su enfoque combina lo contemporáneo, lo lúdico y una base de ideas innovadoras, explorando la memoria y la sostenibilidad. Han ganado varios premios de diseño, destacándose por su originalidad.
Monique Woodward, directora creativa, es arquitecta registrada (ARBV), fellow del Australian Institute of Architects (FRAIA) y consejera nacional del mismo instituto. Scott Woodward, por su parte, es director de proyectos y arquitecto con formación en bellas artes y escultura. Ambos enseñan en Monash University y RMIT, promoviendo el impacto de la arquitectura en las ciudades.